wish

Printed in the United States of America

First Printing, 2014

ISBN 978-0-9907735-0-4

Dancing Poodle Press

www.dancingpoodlepress.com

Cover Photograph © Grier Cooper

Cover Design by LJ Anderson - Mayhem Cover Creations

Formatting by Mayhem Cover Creations

advance praise

"An extremely touching, heartfelt, and often humorous account of a young woman's journey to live her passion. WISH reminds us, that despite our obstacles, we can live the life we dream. You won't be able to put it down."
– *Zippora Karz, Former Soloist, New York City Ballet*
Author of The Sugarless Plum/ Ballerina Dreams

"Grier Cooper expertly weaves her insider knowledge into this compelling read. Even if you've never danced en pointe, you may find yourself reaching for ballet slippers after reading Wish."
– *Charity Tahmaseb, co-author of The Geek Girl's Guide to Cheerleading*

"Grier Cooper's WISH contrasts the elegant and disciplined beauty of ballet versus a gritty and often violent home life. She handles the topic of alcoholism with poignancy and honesty and choreographs in light-hearted moments of friendship, sibling rivalry and a budding romance to round out this touching story of art and love."
- *Paula Yoo (Good Enough, HarperCollins)*

"Grier Cooper writes with emotional hooks that penetrate deeply. Her wonderfully-flawed characters are unforgettable. This book and its lovely dancing protagonist sparkle as if onstage!"
–*Corina Vacco, author of My Chemical Mountain*

"I absolutely loved WISH; it brought back such memories of high school, boys and ballet. What a gift this is to young dance students."
– *Lauren Jonas, Artistic Director, Diablo Ballet*

Table of contents

For my father, Jay Cooper, for always believing in me

chapter one

When I hear the voice I have come to hate, I stop what I'm doing. It doesn't matter that I'm right in the middle of abdominal crunch number 38. This gets preference. I roll on my side and press my ear to the floor. It's hard to hear things through the carpet—more difficult to distinguish the subtle nuances I've learned to listen for—but I don't have a choice. My body tenses as I strain to hear, listening to catch important clues. Is the voice sharp, scratchy and impatient? Bitter and dark? Or round and cloyingly sweet? These things matter. Each one dictates a different course of action.

Another voice responds. But which one? I can't tell. The voice gets louder and I sit up, prepared to move quickly. The volume reaches a crescendo, and I jump into place by the doorway. Just in case. Loud words ring up through the floor below my feet. I stop breathing. Something clatters to the floor with a loud, metallic clank.

I hear a scratching sound. I realize with a start that it's my nails digging into the wooden grooves of the doorframe.

I hold my breath until things go quiet again. After I wait one full minute (again, just in case) I lie down on the floor again. I know I should finish exercising but it feels good to lie still for a moment. Truth be told, I hate abdominal crunches. I close my eyes and a fragment of memory surfaces: a favorite moment from a long time ago, back before my brothers were born, when I flew. I'm not kidding. I remember my body floating weightless, toes hovering several inches above the intricate paisley patterns in our front hall carpet; dust motes twinkled in the sunlight like tiny golden fairies swirling all around me.

It was over too soon. The good stuff always is. But in those few sparkly moments I was free in a way I have never felt since.

When the memory fades, I force myself to do my last round of crunches. The overly bright pink carpet beneath me scratches the bare skin at the nape of my neck but I grit my teeth and continue. My abdominal muscles are on fire and I latch on to that fact. It's proof that something I'm doing is having an effect somewhere.

Sometimes when things get bad, I close my eyes and imagine that blissful flying feeling in my body again. My cells remember. That's how I know it must have happened. The closest I've gotten to that feeling again is during the final moments of ballet class when I leap across the floor. Those few milliseconds of freedom where I defy gravity – the chance to fly – that's what keeps me coming back to the ballet studio.

Lately, I don't ever want to leave.

I hope this is the year Miss Roberta takes me to audition for the New York School of Ballet so I can finally start my real life. But the second I think this, the doubts slither in. Am I ready? What about my brothers? Right now there are no answers, only questions and conflicting feelings.

A droplet of sweat rolls down my right temple and trickles into my ear. I shake it off and finish my last crunch, then flop back on the floor. I imagine what I look like from above: a cast-off rag doll, forgotten and tossed aside.

I stand and take one last look in the mirror. As usual there are a few stray flyaway hairs. I scowl at them and glue them into place with a final spritz of hairspray. That's as close to perfect as my bun is going to get today.

The voice is back, muddled with irritation. This time I'm in the crosshairs. Mom yells again, just in case I didn't hear her the first time. It's impossible not to, even though she doesn't believe in occupying the same room as the person she's talking to.

I grab my ballet bag and fly down the stairs. I know better than to keep her waiting.

Seven blocks before we reach the ballet studio she is screaming so loudly that I see her larynx. Wait. That's not the right word. What is the word...you know, for that dangly thing you always see vibrating in cartoon characters' throats when they yell? The uvula. That's the word. Only this is no cartoon – it's my life.

I see all the signs that a blowup is coming: tight jaw, white knuckles on the steering wheel, growling about every little thing that's bothering her. Usually I jump in and smooth things over, but not this time.

"I'm sick to death of picking up after a houseful of pigs! I'm so goddamned tired all the time because of you!" Mom yells.

Her hands pound the steering wheel and my stomach twists with a sick, fluttery feeling. It's like the world has suddenly spun out of control and there's no solid ground under my feet. I should be used to this by now – I've had almost sixteen years of practice.

My head droops like a wilted flower and I stare at my lap. I shut my eyes. It's so hot in the car that my thighs are sticking to the blue leather seats. I hate that.

I have to escape. My mother is driving me crazy.

I ask myself why this keeps happening. I know she hates driving. Plus today, her lead-footed determination fell short by a few seconds and she missed the light at that one intersection on Post Road where you have to wait an eternity before the light turns green again. Charlie left his towel on the bathroom floor this morning; that kind of stuff always pisses her off. Maybe she's just having a bad hair day. It's Saturday and she's not due back at the hairdresser's until Wednesday morning. All of these things add up, heat her inner coil until it boils over and spills out ugly words.

On the outside my mother looks like an old-school movie star – polished blonde perfection, hair always in a flawless twist – but lately she's wound up like a tightly coiled snake on the inside, ready to strike at any moment. When I think of her, competing emotions swirl around in my ribcage: disappointment, anger, fear and something else – longing. For the person she used to be, a person who now makes occasional cameo appearances. Sometimes I feel sorry for her, but watching her now, her contorted screaming face, (uvula shimmying back and forth like a bobble-headed hula dancer on crack) all sympathy evaporates.

I need to get out of this car to focus on my body, to feel the cool metal ballet barre in my hand. If Mom doesn't stop yelling soon I'll be late for class and Miss Roberta will have my head. I'm tuning it out for now, like watching a movie without sound. Watching without listening almost makes it comical. Like noticing the uvula thing.

She jabs a well-manicured, red-lacquered finger in the air (religiously re-manicured every Tuesday morning) and Charlie cries louder. Poor kid gets blamed for just about everything since he was the mistake, the unplanned child. He's too small to stick up for himself so I try to protect him as often as I can. I squeeze his little hand three times, our secret sign. *I love you and it'll be okay.* He scoots in closer to my side.

Brad rolls his eyes at me from the front seat and smirks. I ignore him and stare at my reflection in the window, hating my strawberry blonde hair and pale skin, all the parts of me that look like her.

Here's another tactic: only listen to every third word she says. Using this filter, the dialogue goes something like, "Christ... goddamn... ever-loving... useless... godforsaken... dirty... you... tired... enough." I've edited out most of the obscenities. Seriously, half of what my mother says would be censored by the FCC. Pretty ironic, since she went to Catholic school from kindergarten through senior year. The woman was practically raised by nuns.

She'll eventually exhaust herself and tell my dad what crappy kids we are the second she gets home. Dad will do what he usually does, which is nothing. Or he'll go work in the yard so he doesn't have to deal with it. Until next time. Lather. Rinse. Repeat.

Charlie's scream pulls me from my thoughts. My

eyes snap open. My mother grips him by the arm as she shakes him, hard. "Another goddamn mess to clean up. Like I don't have enough already." Charlie's cries turn to sobs. I notice scuff marks from his shoes on the back of Mom's seat.

"Great, just great," she growls.

Not right, not right, not right, says a little voice inside me as my heart races frantically. I can't let her hurt him.

"Mom, you can't—"

"Shut. Up." She whips her head towards me, eyes blazing. "Do not start with me or I swear to God I will make you regret it. Just try me and you will find yourself out of ballet classes so fast your head will spin."

The words hover in the air, followed by a sudden blistering silence. A door slams shut in the center of my chest. I fight back the leaden weight of anger and panic with slow, steady breaths. I wish I could make her stop freaking out all the time. But how? I clench my fists, digging the nails into my palms to stifle any urge to respond.

At last she guns the accelerator and drives the final few blocks to the ballet studio. The car rolls to a stop and she eyes each of us in turn. Slowly she turns back toward me. "All right," she says. "Get out."

chapter Two

I feel all weird and shaky as I climb out of the car. I close the door and lean against it with my head bowed. I take a deep breath. I have to pull it together before I go to class. Not easy to do when you have liquid hate pulsing through your veins.

"Indigo, is that you?" a voice says out of nowhere.

Crap. It's Mrs. Davis. Her blonde wavy hair is shellacked into place, her perfectly shaped eyebrows arched in excitement. My heart sinks even further. I swear she and Mom have a secret arranged marriage thing planned for me and Ryan Davis, the maniac perverted son I was forced to play with all through grade school. He spent every one of our play dates either beating me up or trying to look under my dress.

She eyes me up and down like I'm the main course for supper. "I'm so happy to run into you. I have a favor to ask."

Dread keeps me rooted in place, paralyzed. *Must escape before it's too late.* Behind me I hear the car window glide down. I turn to see Mom leaning across the front seat to angle herself into the discussion.

"Why, Pam, how nice to see you." My mother's voice oozes with syrupy sweetness. She's talking in that nice phony voice she only uses when we're out in public. We call it her Christmas voice. It's as fake as the rat poison disguised as sweetener that all the skinny moms in town stir into their morning lattés. No one would ever guess that only moments ago she was screaming her head off at us in the car.

"Likewise, Elizabeth. How are your boys doing?"

"Busy with hockey, as always. And yours?" Mom's voice now has a slight Southern twang to it, as it does when she's laying it on extra thick.

"Same. But you know, I was just about to talk to Indigo about tutoring my Lila; she's behind in reading. I think learning from an older girl she looks up to would do her a world of good."

Before I can stop her, Mom says, "Well, of course, she'd love to help out. Wouldn't you, Indigo?"

No reason to ask me what I think.

They both look at me expectantly. Mom's lips are pressed together in a tight line, a sure sign that she expects no argument from me.

"Uh, sure, Mrs. Davis," I say.

"Oh, fantastic, honey. Thank you so much. How about first thing next Saturday morning, at your place? I'll pay you ten dollars an hour. Oh, Lila will be thrilled!"

I can't believe how easily I just got roped into tutoring Lila. That's the thing about this town: it's impossible to go anywhere without running into someone you know, and usually it's the person you were hoping to avoid.

The Christmas voice echoes in my head as I climb the stairs to Miss Roberta's ballet studio. It's only when I reach the top of the stairs that I realize my hands are gripped into tight fists and my jaw is sore from gnashing my teeth together. I unclench my fingers and shake out my hands, imagining I'm flinging off the bad juju.

The smooth leather texture of my ballet slippers is comforting as I slip my feet into them. I throw on leg warmers and look for a spot at the barre. There's one last spot, right next to Marlene James, ex-fourth grade best friend, now turned horrible person. Lovely.

Monique gives me a questioning look from her spot three places down at the barre, but I shake my head and look away. While I mechanically prepare for class, I don't talk to anyone. I'm still too upset. I throw my right leg up on the barre and fold my body over it, then switch to the left. A thorough full-body stretch is a must before every class, but thanks to my mother that's all I have time for today.

"All right, girls, let's get started," Miss Roberta says, clapping her hands loudly.

I hold the barre lightly with my left hand and begin moving when the music starts. It's the same music I've heard in every ballet class I've taken for the past ten years. We always start with pliés.

My knees bend in time to the music: demi plié, demi plié, grand plié. My body moves through the positions while my mind replays the scene in the car. The image of my mother's uvula is stuck in my brain.

"Indigo, where is your focus this morning?" Miss Roberta's voice pulls me back into the present moment. I glance in front of me at Marlene's feet and realize I'm in the wrong position. I shake my head to clear it. *Go away, Mom. This is the one place where I get away from you – even if it's only for an hour and a half.*

Compared to the rest of my life, ballet classes are refreshingly orderly and predictable. Barre exercises always follow the same routine. Do everything that works the right leg, then turn and repeat everything with the left.

We move through the barre exercises. Every beat of the music dictates what comes next. The rhythm makes demands and the body answers with precision. Already my muscles are beginning to feel warm and stretchy.

"Monique, your leg does not end at your ankle. Point those toes! Jeanine, you're sagging. Stand up straight!" Miss Roberta's voice carries through the room. Today she's all in pinks with a floral chiffon headscarf. She's the classic tiny dancer: dark-haired with pert features. Her eyes flicker across the class, constantly appraising technique and posture. Even though she's tiny, she commands the room. If she sees imperfections or lack of good effort, she will call you out.

Moments later we are doing grand battements. Droplets of sweat roll down my back and the sides of my face. My extensions suck today; my leg just won't go as high as usual. I'm straining to get it up near my shoulder when it's usually as high as my head. Everything feels heavy.

"What is going on with your extensions today, Indigo?" Miss Roberta looks disturbed. She addresses the room. "All of you are operating at half speed. Can anyone tell me why?"

"Must be how hard they're working us in PE at school," Monique pipes in.

"Great, just great. Those people have no idea what havoc they are wreaking on my dancers. Do you girls have to kill yourselves in *gym class*?" Her lips curl like she sucked on a lemon. Miss Roberta is extremely cautious about this stuff. In her world, dancers shouldn't do half the stuff that other normal people enjoy. Skiing, for instance. She has forbidden me to ski because I could break a leg. The list of things I'm not allowed to do gets longer all the time.

"The human body is naturally lazy, girls. You have to make it work for you," Miss Roberta reminds us. This is the first of the "Rules of Ballet According to Miss Roberta." The complete manifesto goes something like this:

Humans are naturally lazy and dancers have to work hard to overcome this tendency.

There is always room for improvement. If you think you are a good enough dancer, you're wrong!

There will always be someone who is a better dancer than you.

It takes hard work and discipline to get ahead.

If you can't take constructive criticism, you are in the wrong place.

If you are too tall, too fat or too lazy, pick a different career.

The love of dance brought you here and it will carry you through your career.

Ballet is equal parts dedication, inspiration, and perspiration.

The human body is a dancer's most important tool and our biggest challenge (see Rule #1).

Ballet involves sacrifice (of certain dangerous activities...including and most especially boys).

"Girls, get the lead out. Let's see some energy in those leg extensions. Make your bodies obey!" Miss Roberta is not known for her subtlety. Also, she is perfectly comfortable discussing touchy subjects, such as personal hygiene. Three years ago she alerted us about the need for deodorant by making a loud public statement in the middle of class that went something like, "Many of you girls are old enough now that you need to wear deodorant. Some of you are beginning to smell."

We put on pointe shoes and practice more relevés and turns at the barre. Turns are all about balance and spotting. I spot the back of Marlene's head in front of me each time I turn. It's a dance secret; the key to spinning around without getting dizzy. Keep your eyes on a single spot as you start to spin, then whip your head around quickly and find the same spot again.

Marlene is an amazing turner. Today I want to hate her, but it doesn't matter anyway, since she probably won't get much further in ballet with those D-cups of hers.

I yank my attention back to turns. It's nerve-wracking, spinning around multiple times on the tip of a pointe shoe. You're balancing on maybe three square inches of surface space, so you have to focus. It doesn't help that I'm tall; there's more of me to control.

Finally it's time to move to the center of the room. I'm always glad to be done with the barre even though it's where the foundation is built. The steps we repeat over and over again are like words in our dance vocabulary, and once we are in the center we flow into fluid dialogue.

We do more tendus and then an adagio. My body blooms and stretches as I raise one leg to the ceiling. Everything remains still as my bottom foot rotates and I revolve like a living jewelry-box ballerina. The music is painfully slow today. We have to make it look easy, but it isn't.

Miss Roberta demonstrates some quick footwork with the lightness of a flitting sparrow. I watch her and wonder what her career was like. I know she was with the American Ballet Theater in New York City – there are photos and newspaper clippings posted around the studio.

Out of the corner of my eye I see Miss Roberta patrolling the edges of the room, watching while we work. Sometimes I swear I feel her eyes burning into the back of my skull. "Feet together in the sous-sus, Indigo! Imagine you are being sucked up into a straw."

As I dance, I watch my feet in the mirrors that line the front of the room. She's right. They should be tighter. I catch Marlene flashing me a haughty look in the mirror. I watch my feet closely, placing them with care.

"Better. Now apply that same diligence to every step you take."

That's a tall order for me today, but I know she's right. I have to maintain that same level of care if I'm going to make it as a dancer. Each time I'm here, my job is to move one more step closer to perfection. And if I get my wish, I won't always have her around to remind me.

For now, Miss Roberta is part mentor, part mother and part tormentor. She embodies the strength and willpower I'll need to get ahead, and she reminds me relentlessly.

While the second group does the exercise, I go to the side of the room and take off my pointe shoes – just for a moment. I'm starting to get bunions on the outer joints of my big toes. Some days my feet ache so badly I want to cry, but I have to work through the pain. Pointe shoes look beautiful on the outside, all pink and satin. But they are instruments of torture. Cement ball gowns. The music ends so I quickly stuff my feet back inside my shoes and tie the ribbons. Just in time for turns.

"Long spine, Indigo!" Miss Roberta's eyes find mine in the mirror. "Shoulders down, Elizabeth! Chin up!"

Another turn. I spot my eyes in the mirror, turn twice and land. I hate this floor; the linoleum is slippery and I worry about falling. *Only think about turns. No fear.* I imagine an iron spike going down through my supporting shoulder and into the ground. It works. I nail the landing perfectly.

"Good, Indigo. Try for three next time."

We move to the far corner of the room for jumps on the diagonal, the giant leaps that are my favorite. Doing them in pointe shoes is challenging because we're supposed to jump soundlessly. Not easy when you've got cement blocks on your feet.

We end class with a reverence, the same way dancers bow on stage at the end of a show. In class it's a show of respect for our teacher.

"Thank you for your hard work," Miss Roberta

says. I take a deep breath and begin to relax, at last. The feeling I get at the end of class is always warm and yummy. I take a gulp from my water bottle to replace the fluids I lost from all the sweating.

"Indigo, I need to see you a moment," Miss Roberta says quietly.

The other dancers filter out into the dressing area and I step into her "office," the corner where the music player lives. She shuts the divider, closing the studio off from the dressing room. Not a good sign.

Miss Roberta clears her throat. "I know you're working hard." I hold my breath, waiting for her to continue. "But your footwork is still sloppy. Your jumps have improved, but could be stronger and you're still a little loose through your core. You really need to step it up if you intend to audition this year."

It's like a punch to the gut. I stare at the floor in quiet desperation as I hold back tears, nodding at her directives.

Her face softens. "Look, you have all the tools you need at your disposal. But what you do with them and how far you go – that's up to you."

chapter three

Mom is all smiles when I get in the car after class. I eye her warily; this kind of smile from her is usually reason for suspicion. Then I notice she's here without my brothers. Maybe that's why she's grinning.

That, and she probably wants something.

"How was class?" she asks, grin intact.

I mumble something unintelligible and pretend I'm looking for something in my dance bag. I'm not in the mood to talk about anything with her. Especially not after this morning.

"That good, huh?" She gives me an appraising glance. "How about we go to Swirl and get a frozen yogurt. My treat. I'm in the mood for rainbow sprinkles." Her musical laugh fills the car.

If only she were like this more often.

After building ourselves ridiculously small cups of yogurt (mine topped with fruit and a few sprinkles, hers all-out sprinkles with whipped cream), we sit outside on brightly-colored, obscenely uncomfortable metal chairs. The rainbow sprinkles improve my mood, but I'm not about to admit this to her.

"Delicious, huh?" She scrapes around for the final remnants. "Anyway, now that we're out I thought we could swing by Grade A and pick up a few things."

Of course there had to be a catch. Once she starts running errands I'll be held hostage for who knows how long. I'd argue if I thought it would do any good.

The second we enter Grade A my skin immediately breaks out in goose bumps, but the polar climate of the refrigerated aisle feels good after being so sweaty in ballet class. Mom goes one way with the shopping cart; I go in the opposite direction.

1. A quick glance around and you'll notice that Darien, Connecticut is a lot like a living J. Crew ad. You'll never find anyone wandering around in PJs in this store. The women are all dressed like they're at a cocktail party, rather than dealing with mundane matters like the price of poultry. Our neighbor, Mrs. Benson, is a fine example of what I mean. She's in a tight red halter and studded stiletto heels; one of those Darien übermoms, like Martha Stewart meets a Victoria's Secret model.

2. It's not a coincidence that both versions of *The Stepford Wives* were filmed here. Those creepy robot

moms from the movie would fit in perfectly. No joke. There's even a shopping center called Goodwives' Shopping Center just down the road.

I'm browsing for shampoo when I hear it. The Christmas voice back in full swing in the next aisle. My mother is talking to someone. I peek my head around the corner.

She sees me and beams. "Here she is. This is my daughter, the ballerina, the one I was talking about," she says, sweeping her arm in my direction. The stranger nods, looking at the floor. It's hard to say which one of us is more uncomfortable. Probably him; his feet are already turned away, preparing to make a hasty exit.

"Well, then," he says, giving me a confused smile, "it was nice to have met you both. Good luck in New York." He run/walks down the aisle until he's out of sight. Who knows how these conversations start, but it's always the same scenario: Mom ends up talking to them about *my* life.

"What a nice man," she murmurs.

The grocery store is one of her few social outlets and two minutes later she starts gabbing with Mrs. Benson. I decide to look over in the office supply section for some notebooks. I kneel down to look at some cool glittery notebooks on the bottom shelf when, out of the corner of my eye, I see someone stroll by. Actually I only see the shoes. Black steel-toed boots with buckles up the side. Jesse Sanders.

Last summer we had a thing for about five minutes.

There was this end-of-summer beach barbeque, and we ended up talking all night. Since then I only catch occasional glimpses of him in the halls at school.

Luckily he doesn't notice me all hunched over on the floor with my hands full of notebooks. I have to get out of here before he sees me. I've already used up all of my "unexpected encounters" points today.

I stand up quickly and before I know it, my hair (still in a stupid bun) catches on one of those protruding metal hooks used to display packing tape dispensers. They tumble to the floor along with the notebooks that slip from my hands, taking out a whole bunch more stuff as they fall. Packages of labels, tape, markers and pens go flying.

This makes a huge racket. Every head in the store turns to look at me standing in the middle of the mess, eyebrows raised up to my hairline, face stuck in a horrified grimace. Yeah, that's me, the graceful ballerina.

Jesse Sanders rounds the corner a second later.

I call moments like these my "blonde moments" because really, there's no other explanation for them. This one is "blonde moment number 4,327." Ironically, I have spent most of my life training to move with precision and grace, but every now and then I do something incredibly clumsy and embarrassing like this.

"Need a little help?" Jesse says. A smile tugs at the corner of his mouth as he bends down to pick up the notebooks.

He has dimples. Oh God. I forgot he has dimples.

"You think?" I say, laughing nervously. *God, I sound like a hyena.*

He leans in to unhook my hair and I catch his scent, citrus and spice. My eyes fall on the necklace lying against the exposed skin of his chest. It's a giant tooth or claw set into a silver spiral. I imagine how warm it is from touching his skin and I feel my face flush.

No time for boys, Indigo. I turn away with a jerk and sort the mess into neat piles.

The store manager shows up. "Okay, move along," he says, scowling. "You've done enough here."

"Does this mean we're eighty-sixed from shopping here ever again?" I ask as we scurry away.

Jesse looks back over his shoulder. "That guy has a serious rod up his…"

I smile. "Hey, thanks for the help." My smile fades when I notice my mother looking for me. Must. Run. Away. Before she comes over here and says something embarrassing. "Okay, well, see ya!" I run off and leave him standing there, still holding the stack of notebooks.

I'm breathing hard when I reach my mom. She looks at my empty hands quizzically. "I thought you were going to get some notebooks."

"Yeah, I just couldn't decide."

"All right, then. We're out of here."

It's the best thing she's said to me all day.

chapter four

I hate being late but I hate being late on Mondays most of all. By the time Becky's car comes into view I can tell it's going to be one of those Mondays. Her car is easy to spot from a distance but it's hard to say exactly what color it is. The paint job is all 80s neon-orange gone bad, mottled over time by repeated applications of spray paint.

Becky's all in earth tones today: fringed caramel suede jacket, burgundy brocade pants with a velvet vest, and feathered earrings dangling from sparkly chains.

Before I've even buckled my seatbelt, Monique leans forward and squeals in my ear while she hugs me.

"Ow. That was my ear. How can you be so rowdy

this early?" I say.

She laughs. "My top secret formula: triple-shot latté." She's been going off the deep end with caffeine experiments ever since her mom bought a cherry-red, top-of-the-line espresso maker.

"You might want to ease up a little on your caffeine intake."

"We can't all be as pure as the driven snow like some people around here," she retorts.

A muffled voice from the backseat says, "Whose bogus idea was it to start school at 7:45 am? As in *before* 8:00 am?" Sarah's face is smooshed into a pillow, half-hidden by her long blonde curls.

I glance at the clock on the dash and sigh. We are going to be late, which makes me crazy. Probably because timeliness is one of the few areas of my life where I have any control. Becky is one of those time-challenged people who don't have a concept of how much time it takes to get things done. Unfortunately, she's also the only one of us with a driver's license.

My temples throb. I eye the beaded dream catcher swinging from the rearview mirror and remind myself to breathe.

"Did you finish that map for Dunlop last night?" Sarah says, stifling a yawn.

"Don't do that. It's contagious," I warn. "I finished it days ago. I showed it to you Friday, remember?"

"Guess it slipped my mind. I had practice last night so I barely got mine done and I'm pretty sure it sucks."

Sarah joined a soccer team last season, not because she loves the sport but because of its social prospects. All she talks about these days is boys and soccer.

I sigh and look away. The clock now says we are supposed to be at school in seven minutes. "We are going to be so late," I whine.

"Relax. I know it's a four-letter word for you but you can do it." Monique gives me her patented one-arched-eyebrow stare-down.

Sarah prattles on. "So then Sean asked me out for Friday and I was like, okay, yeah I'll go with you, and then he walked away and I was totally kicking myself because I didn't want to go with him, like, anywhere actually." She rolls her eyes dramatically. The others nod in sympathy.

"But then, like five minutes later, Tommy shows up and he asks me out for Friday. And I don't know why, but I said yes to him, too."

"Girl—" Monique says.

"I know, right?" Sarah's voice is heavy with guilt. "So then he went away all happy and I was, too, for like a second, and then I was like, oh crap, what have I done?"

Becky shakes her head. "And then?"

"Well, Sean showed up again like five minutes after that…he was so pissed his eyes were bugging out. He totally yelled at me and then stormed off." She sighs. "I mean, I couldn't blame him, right?" Another sigh. "I don't know why I said yes to him in the first place. Now they aren't talking to each other."

This earns her a collective groan from the group.

"I know. So beat." She digs around in her backpack and holds up a paper bag. "Bagels, anyone? Fresh from Anthony's. Anyone?" She passes them around to multiple outstretched hands. "What, nothing for you, Indigo? Are you *sure*?"

I shake my head. "Thanks, but I can't." Not if I plan to stay thin.

"No bagels? How sad." She makes an exaggerated sad face. "Okay then, you know you're missing out." She takes a huge bite, closes her eyes and moans.

I want to smack her. "Not helping. Totally the opposite, in fact." I sit there feeling pissy. Somewhere, some part of me is dying for a bagel. Or a little fun, for that matter. A break in the heavy fog of life.

One good thing. I need one good thing to happen to me.

We arrive with seconds to spare.

"Indigo, wait up!" Jesse leans up against the row of lockers. His muscled arms are beautiful in the blue T-shirt he's wearing.

This isn't what I meant, God. I need my one good thing to be something that won't mess up my other good thing.

We stand only a few feet apart while people rush through the space between us. Part of me wants to just keep walking and pretend I didn't hear him. But then I have this thought that says *hear him out...what if this* is *your one good thing?*

I don't know why I would think that.

I shake my head and look up. Our eyes meet. Well, sort of. More like I glance at his eyes and then stare at his shoulder.

"Hi." My voice is strangely hoarse.

"Hey, I just wanted to ask if you—"

The bell cuts him off. That decides things for me. I shrug helplessly. Then I bolt.

It's always cold in the rank locker room, regardless of the season. I struggle into my crappy PE uniform, a unitard with navy and white stripes on the top half and navy shorts on the bottom.

"Why do our uniforms look like they were designed for Florida jailbirds?" I say. "I hate putting this thing on. It's totally polyester trying to disguise itself as cotton."

Monique sits on the bench nearby, smirking, as I thrust my arms into the sleeves.

"Really, people, whose brilliant idea was this? We live in the Northeast, which means that for more than half the year this uniform makes absolutely no sense."

We jog out to the far field that backs up against Willow Grove Cemetery. The headstones in the distance look like rows of teeth ruptured out of the ground.

"All right, girls, circle up!" Ms. Miller blows her whistle for attention. "Today we're running! Sprints first, then long distance! You will be timed!" In her world, every statement ends with an exclamation point.

"I am so not up for this," Monique grumbles.

I bend forward, stretching my hamstrings. "I know. Miss Roberta will kill us if we come into class wrecked again."

She slides into a lunge, grimacing. "Tell me about it. Last week she yelled at me because I totally hurt myself in the long jump. My thighs were so sore I could hardly walk for a week."

"Stevens! You're up!" Just then, Coach Foster runs past us with a group of guys. Jesse's at the head of the line.

Don't look, don't look, don't look...

I stare at my sneakers. But the more I try not to look at him the more my eyes feel pulled that way, like a giant magnetic force has taken over.

He lifts his right hand in a wave as he passes us. Marlene James sees the whole thing and stares at me, her eyes narrowing into menacing slits.

"Um, what was that?" Monique stage-whispers. She's so close to my right shoulder that she's practically sitting on it.

"That was nothing," I say.

"It was a subtle nothing, I'll give you that. But it looked more like a something to me."

"Trust me. It was nothing and that's all it ever will be." I fold my arms, indicating that the conversation is over.

"Stevens! Let's go!!" Ms. Miller screeches.

I hate running. I'm not a runner, and I don't want to be. But I feel the guys watching our every move. I take off and push as hard as I can. Soon the sweat starts flowing and my breath kicks up a few notches to keep time with the steady beat of my feet. I run like I'm trying to escape from something. Or someone.

When Ms. Miller finally blows her whistle, I push on. My lungs burn as I run inside without looking back.

We meet at our usual table for lunch, just outside the doors to the kitchen. Loud clanging noises come from inside the kitchen.

"What are they doing in there?" Becky asks.

"Probably fighting back. The food is trying to crawl out of the warming trays," Sarah says.

Mr. Peters, the western civics teacher, saunters over to our table. Shifty-eyed and oily, his hair always looks like it might slither off at any moment. He blinks at us through huge glasses with thick black frames. He points to Becky's hot dog and says, "You know what those are made of? Lips and assholes, my friends, lips and assholes." He grins slyly before adding, "It's still beef, though."

He saunters off and we all stare at the hot dog. "That's it," Becky sputters. "He has single-handedly destroyed my love for hot dogs."

"Change of subject?" Sarah says.

"Jesse Sanders is hot for Indigo," Monique offers.

"Is not." I sound so mature.

"Say more about this," Becky says to Monique.

"There's nothing to tell," I protest.

Sarah is the only one who isn't staring at me.

Time for another change of subject. "Who are you texting?" I ask her.

"Tommy Wilson." She doesn't look up as she answers.

Monique snorts. "Tommy Wilson who's sitting two tables away? Are you kidding me?"

"Some people find it amusing to text like this."

"Some people meaning *Tommy*." Monique is clearly exasperated. But at least she's focused on something besides me.

Sarah sighs. "You wouldn't understand."

I use this moment to leave.

I run into Mr. Levinson on the stairs. "Indigo! Just the person I wanted to see!" His round face beams behind wire-rimmed spectacles that are a little too tight for his face.

I smile back. "Hi, Mr. L." He's one of the few people around here that I actually enjoy.

He guides us to the side of the stairs to let other

people pass. "I'm putting together the final roster for the winter concert. I wanted to see if I could talk you into dancing that night."

My mouth starts to say no, but then I spy Marlene James coming down the stairs with her entourage. She slows down and stares at me, little daggers of hate flying from her eyes. I angle my body so I don't have to look at her. And then it occurs to me. It would be foolish to turn down an opportunity – any opportunity – to perform. Even at school. What if this is my one good thing?

"Sure, Mr. L., I'll do it. That would be awesome."

He clasps his hands in delight. "Great. Great! I'll put you down then. See you later." He pats my shoulder and then he's gone.

"*Sure, Mr. L., I'll do it. That would be awesome.*" Marlene's voice is ripe with sarcasm. Her minions laugh. "God, give me a break. Like anyone here wants to see you parading around in a leotard."

"Go pluck your eyebrows. I think you missed one." I shove past her.

"You think that's going to impress Jesse?" she screams after my retreating back. "You've got another thing coming!"

But she doesn't know there's only one thing I care about: dancing my way out of here.

chapter five

I've noticed this thing keeps happening when I get home. The second I put my hand on the doorknob, I don't want to go in. Today when I open the back door all I see is a thick wall of smoke. A few steps later I see why: Mom's sitting in her "office," the little round table we have in the kitchen by the phone. Her feet are propped up on the table, right next to her green glass ashtray. It's overflowing with butts.

Normally she naps in the afternoons, but no such luck today.

"I'm telling you, Lorraine, you should have been there," she says. She waves the hand holding her cigarette. The ash is so long it dangles by a thread. She pauses to take a long drag on her cigarette, then puffs the smoke out the side of her mouth. The ash falls on the table but she doesn't notice.

Lorraine Rausch is one of Mom's two closest friends. They talk on the phone almost daily; for at least 45 minutes.

Mom scowls at her cigarette. "I couldn't believe the balls on this guy." Her voice gets louder. "So I told him to stuff it."

I grab Monique's elbow. "Let's just go upstairs the other way." I start walking.

"Hi, sweetie. You're home early, aren't you?" She waves her hand overenthusiastically. "Monique, so great to see you, too, love." Mom's voice is so sweet it could erode tooth enamel. I grit my teeth and pray she stops talking.

This is why I don't bring friends home.

She turns her attention back to the phone. "Sorry about that, Lorraine. Indigo and her friend just walked in the door. I know—"

The tight feeling in my stomach doesn't let up, even after we've escaped to my room. I close the door and sink on the bed. I look around my room, hating everything about it. I'm tired of the plain white walls, the fuchsia carpet, the loud floral drapes and matching bedspread. I sigh. Am I just hyperaware of my mother's behavior or is she truly an aberration?

"So what's up with your mom?" The question comes just as I'm starting to relax. So much for Monique not noticing my freaky mother.

I stare at the ceiling. Unfortunately there are no answers written there. "She's always like that when she talks with her friends."

"Does she drink a lot of coffee?"

I roll my eyes and bury my face in the pillow. The girl can't stop talking about coffee.

"Whatevs. Just wondering." She shrugs and starts flipping through my CDs.

Maybe I'm just tired of living within these walls, regardless of their color.

"What is it with you and the CDs? MP3s are easier," Monique says.

A lot of my music is classical. I listen to the music I dance to as often as I can, especially when I'm gearing up to perform. "This music is timeless. Who cares what form it's in?"

Monique yawns loudly in response. "I'm parched. Got anything to drink around here?"

Just what I want, another journey into Christmas voice territory. I force a smile. "I'll go check. You can chill here."

I creep downstairs. Luckily Mom's still on the phone. I scan the shelves. Mom keeps everything hyper-organized in here since we use it for laundry and storage. It's full of cleaning products, snacks, drinks, batteries, and light bulbs; all in perfect rows. Somehow she'll notice if anything is an inch out of place.

I grab a bottle of sparkling water and hastily pour it into two cups. I consider adding ice. Screw the ice. The machine is way too loud.

I hear snippets of her conversation: "I wish I knew, Lorraine. But he couldn't tell me any more than that."

Must not eavesdrop. I reach up and slide the bottle back into place.

"Yes, I know it's serious, Lorraine. It isn't every day you find out you've only got a few months to live."

I freeze, not daring to move.

"I'm going to tell Jake tonight. We'll have to figure out together how to tell the kids." A pause. "I don't know if we should tell the kids."

I freeze in place and stifle a sob. The floor creaks loudly under my feet.

"Indy?" her voice calls out. "Is that you?"

I slowly slither up the stairs and creep away even though something inside me says to run. I almost trip on the top step but catch myself at the last second. Water pours from the cups and slops onto the floor. I watch the bubbles pop, one after the next, like lights burning out one by one.

I sit down heavily on the top step. I try to take a deep breath but I can't. Fear is a crushing vice around my chest. My breathing is erratic, full of ragged edges. After who knows how many moments, I stand. Paste on a normal face.

"Took you long enough," Monique says when I return. "Did you go to the store or something?" She lazily rearranges her limbs on my bed and reaches for the glass I offer her.

"Nah. Nature called." I laugh but it comes out shaky and fake.

I set down my cup and walk over to the window. The trees outside are an explosion of fall color: red, amber, gold, deep burgundy. The color of blood.

Like the world is on fire.

chapter six

It's an inky black night. Darkness hovers outside the windows like it's clamoring to get in and suck our souls away. It always feels weird to be at school at night. Or maybe that's just me being grumpy about spending more time here.

I tried to talk to Mom before she dropped me at rehearsal, but she was freaking out about getting back since she'd left my brothers home alone. Now the worry creeps back. While I stretch, I watch the chorus. My muscles are warm but I feel cold.

"With feeling, people! Reach into your guts!" Mr. Levinson is passionate about his work. He sang with the New York Opera but his career ended when he pushed his voice too hard during an illness and damaged his vocal chords. Although listening to him now you'd never know.

The chorus is a strangely eclectic blend of nerds, kids from the popular crowd, and straight-up stoners – people who normally wouldn't be caught dead together. Of course, the minute rehearsal ends they will scatter like roaches under bright light. For now they do exactly as Mr. L. says. Everyone does; he is that kind of guy.

I let the music wash over me in a wave as I stretch and relevé to force warmth into my cold, tight calves to make them pliable for jumps and landings. I wish for a split second that I'd chosen an easier variation, something I could hit confidently every time. But there wasn't enough time to start from scratch and pull together a new one. Maybe this will push me to reach higher and develop my strength. Either way, it's good to perform. I always feel like something is missing when I'm not performing.

Mr. L. claps loudly, signaling the end of the chorus rehearsal. "All right people, see you next week. Same bat time, same bat channel." The group evaporates within seconds, as predicted.

"Ready to do this thing, Indigo?" Mr. L. smiles broadly. His smiles are contagious, and I find myself smiling back.

"Sure, Mr. L." I pull off my sweatpants and take my starting position onstage.

"Let me just be sure the music is cued up." He pushes a few buttons and music blares out at an ear-splitting level. We both jump, covering our ears. He hits another button. "Yikes! Sorry." He shakes his head. "All right. Now we're set."

I strike an arabesque en pointe and feel strength zip through the long lines of my body. Right away I notice the floor on this stage is even more slippery than the one at Miss Roberta's. I wish I'd thought to bring rosin. For now I make my steps tinier and more careful.

Out of the corner of my eye, I see Mr. L. and rows of empty auditorium seats. I run to the back corner for a turning sequence. When I face the front again there's a figure in the doorway.

Jesse lounges against the wall. His uniform and hair glisten with sweat. A flash of heat rises to my face and a chill runs up my spine. I feel naked and exposed up here, alone in my leotard. It's ten times worse than being at the beach in a bikini. Leotards show *everything*. I shake the thought away.

Instead I count my turns. Seven more to go. I whip my head to spot each turn, using his blurry form as my focus point, imagining I'm shaking off all thoughts of him.

It doesn't work. I strike another pose and sneak a look at his face. With each turn I feel more and more like I'm on display. I don't want him here. It's screwing me up.

The final flurry of chaîné turns carries me across the stage, seconds away from my final arabesque. I'm breathing hard and my limbs go quivery. I am angry with him and with myself for caring, but my stupid heart has a mind of its own.

I hit a slippery patch and my front foot slips out from under me. I skid across the floor and catch myself just before I end up in the splits. The music ends. I feel dazed from the near fall.

"Are you okay, Indigo?" Mr. L's face pleats with concern.

"No...I mean...yes. I'm fine." I keep my eyes on the floor, too afraid to own my shame in front of Jesse.

"You sure?"

I nod. When I finally work up the courage to look at the doorway, it's empty.

When I leave school, the stars and moon are crystal clear overhead. The chill in the night air stabs at the damp parts of my body. It's such a sudden contrast from inside that I shiver. I hug myself and run my hands up and down my arms to get warm. It's not enough, so I jump up and down in place and inwardly curse my dad for being late.

The door slams behind me and I immediately stop jumping. So I'll be a little less warm. At least I won't look like a freak.

"Don't stop. It was kind of cute." Jesse's voice is warm with laughter. At least something is warm out here.

"It's not a show," I tell him. "I'm trying to stay warm." I cross my arms tightly.

"Here. Let me help you," he says, throwing out an arm to wrap around me.

I hold up both hands in protest and back away. "No thanks. You're all sweaty."

"And you're not?"

He has a point. "Good point."

"It's nice to be right every once in a while." He grins and slides his hands in his coat pockets.

I peer down the road. There's no sign of Dad. Hello, awkward silence. Where the heck is Dad when I need him?

"So, you were good in there."

"Oh God. Please. That was a disaster."

"Seriously. You were awesome. I mean, I don't know anything about ballet so I don't exactly know what I'm talking about. But I do know good when I see it."

"Thanks."

More silence.

Aaagh. "Um…" *Brilliant opening, Indigo. You go, girl.* "So, when is your next game?"

"Friday. You should come."

Headlights appear and we both turn our heads. The car screeches to a stop inches away from our feet. The passenger window rolls down. "Hurry up and get in," Mom says. "Mrs. LaRue is watching your brothers. We have to jet." It's the freaking Christmas voice.

She eyes Jesse. "Oh," she says. "Who do we have here?"

Why me? "Mom, you know Jesse. Jesse Sanders.

Remember?"

"Right." Her hand flies to her mouth dramatically, like she's starring in her own private soap opera. She giggles. "Of course I do."

I quickly get in. "We should go. Right, Mom?"

She giggles again. I roll my eyes as I close the window. Jesse smiles sympathetically.

Mom guns it and I fall back against my seat. "How was rehearsal, sweetie?" She swivels her head to look at me.

Right then, I know we are headed for trouble. "Mom! Mom, look out!"

There's a tremendous thud as she drives onto the turnaround island in the middle of the driveway. The car bucks and lurches sideways. My head whips back against the seat rest.

"Jesus, Mom! You just drove on the island!"

She giggles in response. "Now, Indy, you know I don't see well at night."

"Mom, hey! Slow down!"

She doesn't break speed as the car crashes down off the island. She pulls a Hollywood stop on her way out of the driveway, narrowly missing an oncoming car. The driver leans on his horn but she doesn't even seem to notice.

"Are you hungry?" she asks. "Cuz I'm hungry."

I stare at her like the four-wheeling lunatic I now know her to be.

And Jesse saw the whole thing.

Perfect.

chapter seven

The wood creaks as Monique and I scramble down the rickety stairway that leads from the ballet studio to the ground floor. The lights are still off downstairs, which means the little art gallery isn't open yet; they always run late on Saturdays. I love looking around before they open. Viewing the artwork in dim light feels peaceful and reverent. I feel giddy knowing I am free for the rest of the afternoon. I hear music and light overhead; Miss Roberta must be rehearsing something.

"Come check out this painting," Monique whispers. "I love it."

She points to a portrait of a girl with perfect alabaster skin and a blood-red velvet gown, standing in a grove of moss-laden oaks. A raven sits perched on her shoulder.

"Pretty and kind of dark," I whisper back. "Wish my skin looked that good." My eye falls on a painting of a woman in a flowing dress, sleeping in a bed of flowers. "Look at this one."

We stare at it together. "Dreamy," she says. A sidelong glance. "Why are we whispering?"

We erupt into a giggling fit and tumble out into the sunshine. I am momentarily blinded after being in the dark gallery. I put a hand on her shoulder and struggle to catch my breath.

She grows serious. "What got into you this morning? You were on fire in class today."

Because my mother is dying and I am freaking out and class is my only outlet to stay sane.

"I don't know. It was one of those days where everything just clicks, I guess." One of those days where I'm driven to push myself in every leap and turn.

"Wish I had more of those," she says.

I don't. I sigh. "Lunch or bookstore?"

Monique looks up the street. "Bookstore. I'm not hungry yet."

We sidestep a mother with two toddlers and several joggers before we get to Winds of Desire, the town variety store. This place always has a crazy display of wind-driven decorations, all fluttering and twirling in the wind. I've loved coming here ever since I was a kid. For just a second, I'm six again. Life was so much easier then.

"Let's go in. I haven't been here in forever."

Monique sighs. Evidently she's not feeling the magic. "If we have to. For like five minutes."

I leave with a tiny fairy kite trailing behind me as I walk. I slip it into my backpack before we enter Red Fern Books; the place is hazardous even on a good day. The impossibly narrow aisles are crammed with huge towers of used and vintage books perched precariously on tables. More piles weigh down every available sagging shelf. There's treasure to be found here…if you have time to search for it.

Monique heads to the romance section. I look in performing arts. Last time I was here I scored an amazing dance photography book. Today there's nothing interesting except the *Birthday Book*. I open it to my date: it says I have difficulty relaxing and I'm destined to a life of being hard on myself.

Tell me something I don't already know.

I find Monique sitting on the floor, surrounded by a pile of romance novels. I glance at one and snort. "These covers are so overkill. Look at that guy. He's a Neanderthal!"

It's possible I'm biased. We have tons of these books lying around our house. Mom is a member of some dorky romance book club, so we get a carton of them every month.

"You and your bodice rippers," I say.

"One day I will get some action again. Until then, I have my little escapist pleasures." She waves a book at me.

"Gag. If you need me, I'll be in the restroom puking."

"Seriously?" She stares at me, searchingly.

I roll my eyes. "Of course not seriously."

I have to pee so badly I scramble through the crammed aisles. My elbow sends a book flying to the floor. I grab it, throw it back, and keep running. I round the corner and almost collide with someone. Black, steel-toed boots. Buckles up the sides. Jesse. Our faces are inches apart. My stomach flips.

"You in a hurry or something?" Jesse says.

"Um," I mumble, trying desperately not to cross my legs like a Kindergartner.

"I've got to—" I gesture helplessly at the restroom door.

"Oh," he says. "Right. Sure." He steps aside.

I scurry inside, feeling mortified about my human needs. What if he hears me peeing? When I exit the bathroom he hasn't moved. I groan inwardly.

His easy smile makes me relax. A little. "So… what's going on?" he asks.

"Treasure hunting."

"What?"

"You never know what you're going to find here, right?"

"True." He chuckles. "I didn't think I'd find you here."

That makes two of us.

"Actually, I never know when I'll run into you. Like the other night. That was nice. And weird." He looks pensive. "And your mom—"

Alarm bells go off in my brain. I avert my gaze and think about how to change the subject. "It was so cold that night. My toes were popsicles—"

"There you are." Monique materializes next to me.

I look at Jesse and shrug. "We should probably get going." I widen my eyes at Monique.

"Actually…" Monique has a huge grin on her face.

I know what she's going to say before she says it, only I really, really wish she wouldn't.

"We're going to lunch. You should come." Monique's grin is Cheshire.

Say yes. I mean no. He has to say no. Definitely no.

"Can't," he says. "I'm meeting the guys." He looks at his phone. "Already late. Next time, for sure." A quick wink and he's gone.

I watch him lope casually out the door and my body sags with relief.

"I don't know what you're tripping about. It's on with him." Monique chuckles.

"No. Just…no. That's the last thing I need." So then why do my feet feel like they are hovering a few inches off the ground? And this funny, tingly feeling in my chest won't go away.

"Hey. I was standing here. I saw how he was looking at you."

"I don't need distractions. What about New York?"

"I know New York is important, but what about living a little?" Monique puts a hand on my shoulder. "You should see yourself right now. Face it – you are gone, girl."

I shake my head. "This conversation is over." But the tingling says otherwise.

She throws up her hands. "Have it your way. Let's go eat. I'm starved."

When I return home, Mom is in the kitchen arranging a bouquet of roses. Our garden is full of them. Every morning she's out there faithfully feeding them leftover coffee grounds. The sink holds a chaotic jumble of fallen leaves and petals, a rainbow of yellows, vibrant oranges and velvety reds. My mother has always been unapologetic in her use of color; it's one of the only times she is unrestrained.

She hums while she gathers up the pile of prepared roses. Her tune seems mournful in contrast to the color blooming in her hands. Clipping, tucking, humming the dirge she's got looping through her brain, she sets them in the square glass vase and gives them a final sweep with her fingertips before stepping back to admire her work.

Her arrangements are always perfect. While I admire her skill, the metaphor doesn't escape me. She is just like her roses: pretty and prickly.

"Oh, you're home," she says, noticing me noticing her.

"Those look nice," I say as I head inside.

The shower is always my friend. Warm water soothes my muscles and washes away the layer of dried sweat from class. My rebellious mind plays snapshots of Jesse's necklace on the smooth skin near his collarbone. His smile. Those green eyes.

I grab my shower brush and scrub away the thoughts.

After I dry off and moisturize I throw my hair up in a towel, genie-style, and get down to the grimy business of cleaning out my dance bag. I am shocked to see what's living at the very bottom of the bag: a half-eaten protein bar, a tangle of holey hairnets, handfuls of bobby pins and some unidentifiable brown, crumbly detritus. I am too disgusted to even try to identify the source.

I return downstairs, braiding my hair while it's still wet. It's the only way I can get some wave in my stick-straight hair.

I return to the kitchen; then I stop in my tracks. It looks like a floral bomb went off in here. The vase sits dejectedly by the sink. Two remaining flowers droop in mourning for the rest of their companions, which lie decimated in the sink. A confetti of scattered petals decorates the counter and sink, while a few lay randomly on the floor.

Then I notice the pile of naked stems, every petal torn away as if some rabid deer got a hold of them. I stare uncomprehendingly at the mess. My heart thuds in my chest.

My first thought is to turn around and retreat. But I can't. Some invisible force has seized control of my limbs and my feet are sending me to find Mom, half out of morbid curiosity and the distant need to be a caring daughter.

I find her in the living room. She sits zombie-like in Dad's reading chair, staring straight ahead. One hand hangs limply in her lap, and the other is wrapped casually around the glass on the table beside her. Untamed flyaway strands of blonde hair frame her face, giving her a wild look. I don't know why, but I feel afraid.

"Mom?" My voice is a timid croak. Silent moments pass with no sign that she's registered my presence.

I clear my throat. "Mom," I say, more forcefully this time.

She startles like she's been pinched. Her glassy eyes swim languidly. "Indigo," she drawls slowly, like language is foreign on her lips. She absently swirls the drink beside her, ice tinkling in the glass.

I look at her hand wrapped around the frosty glass. I feel cold. "Is everything all right? Your flowers—"

She laughs mirthlessly. "No, Indigo. Everything is *shit*. Complete and utter shit." She glances down at her drink and takes a long pull, draining the liquid from the glass.

I don't know how to respond to this. I blather on. "But your flowers…"

"Fuck the flowers. They are inconsequential when everything else is going down the toilet."

"Like what? I don't understand." I stare at her, wondering what else she isn't telling me.

"You wouldn't understand, Indigo. Maybe one day you will but I sincerely hope you never do."

She walks woodenly to the kitchen. I hear the clink of more ice cubes and liquid gurgling as she pours herself another drink. She reappears in the doorway, leaning on it, stirring her drink with one finger. "Set the table, will you? For four. Your father has to work late tonight. Again." She takes a long shuddery breath. "I'm going to take a bath."

chapter eight

The gym already smells like sweat and feet and the game hasn't even started yet. The crowd is alive with buzzing energy, a competition of chatting voices that sound like a manic flock of honking geese. Luckily, Sarah's wearing her signature vanilla perfume. I scoot a little closer, hoping vanilla is strong enough to overpower the rest.

I turn to Monique. "Your mom is my new favorite person. How did she convince my mom to let me out tonight?" I've never been so grateful to get out of my house.

"My mom talks a good game. I'll give her that," Monique replies.

Now I know where M gets it. Her persuasive

powers are legendary.

I feel a weird prickly sense like I'm being watched. I turn my gaze courtside and sure enough, Marlene James is staring at me with a venomous look on her face. She catches me looking at her and lifts her chin with a little huff before turning away to primp and gossip with the other cheerleaders.

"If a group of us sent her murderous hate-vibes, how many people would we need to make her shrivel?" Monique asks. "Just make sure Marlene stays at least three feet away from me or I can't be held responsible." Marlene told the entire fifth grade when Monique started her period and they've been mortal enemies ever since.

I yawn. "Why did I let you guys talk me into this again?"

Monique wiggles her eyebrows. "I've got two words for you. Hot. Guys." Becky rolls her eyes. Sarah nods enthusiastically.

Right. There is that. For some of us, anyway.

And tomorrow is Saturday and Miss Roberta will kill me if I am not on my game. But I already did my exercises…

Monique lays a hand on my knee. "Indy, I swear to God. You are so itchy, you are bouncing in your seat. It's making me nuts. Will you just relax?"

Relax? Not my strong point.

She puts on a businesslike face. "Seriously. You need to loosen up, girl." She hands me her giant soda cup. "Here, have a sip of this."

"You brought a sippy cup to the game? What are you, five?" I take a sip. It's root beer and...something else. Vodka, I think. Gross. I try to hide the grimace on my face.

"No thanks," I say, handing it back to her. "I'm good." The last thing I need is more alcohol in my life.

I catch a glimpse of Jesse with his team down at the other end of the court. He breaks off from the group and heads over to the sidelines. The muscles in his arm bulge as he tilts back his head to chug water. Okay, so maybe the hot guy theory is part of the reason I'm here after all.

A horn blares and the players take position. There's a wave of movement as everyone leans forward in their seats.

At the whistle, the figures on the court spring into action, shoes squeaking as they sprint, dribble and dodge. I struggle to keep track of red versus blue but it's all a chaotic dance with partners switching places every few seconds. The ball comes down to our side of the court but is quickly hefted back the other way. Back and forth it travels. Then the ball is in Jesse's hands. He darts across a small distance to get under the net. I start to feel dizzy. He shoots. I realize the dizziness is because I have been holding my breath.

The ball arcs toward the net but the other team bats it away at the last moment. Jesse's teammate grabs it and sends it back Jesse's way. The opposition jostles him out of position. He whirls around on the balls of his feet, ducks under random arms blocking his way, and with a powerful thrust of his thighs he is airborne.

I watch him, transfixed as he hurtles toward the apex of his leap. The curve of his throwing arm makes a lazy arc as he gently releases the ball. He has all the grace and power of Mikhail Baryshnikov. Only he's younger, taller, and cuter.

The ball drips off the tips of his fingers and into the net. A deafening cheer roars through the gym as everyone in the entire student body screams their heads off.

I slump onto Sarah's shoulder as relief and post-adrenaline warmth spreads through my limbs.

"Someone's crushing hard," she says, patting my head like a dog.

"Maybe," I admit. "But stop petting me. I'm not a dog."

"No need to get snappy." She shrugs. "I thought you were finally on my wavelength a little."

As if.

But her pouty face wins my sympathy. I grin at her. "I guess you're right."

"Must be my incredible powers of perception." She looks down on the court and sighs.

"So who's the flavor of the week?" I tease.

"Same as last week."

"Get out. Tommy?"

" I *know*. I can't figure out how it happened.

There's this crazy zingy electricity thing between us. I am completely powerless."

"Well, just don't lose your head over him," I remind her, but I'm not sure if I'm talking to her or myself.

I turn my attention back to the court and I wonder if I am under the spell of my own zingy electricity thing.

The post-game parking lot scene is a cacophony of honking horns, testosterone swagger and packs of screaming girls. The four of us link arms and march in unison, dodging cars and public shows of bravado. We skirt past Chris Johnson's ridiculous ride, a red pickup set on wheels three sizes too large. The engine roars to life, spooking Becky. She screams.

Chris's head pops out of the driver's side window. "Sorry, pretty lady!" he says, cackling. He's so not sorry. I fight the urge to smack some of the freckles off his smirking face. He revs the engine again. Jerk.

We give Chris and his wheels a wide berth. Another car skims by us, narrowly missing direct contact.

"Watch it, jerk off!" Becky slips a protective arm around me.

I watch in a daze as the car drives off, then I turn to

Monique. "Where are we supposed to meet your mom again?"

"Hey, Indigo! Wait up!" Jesse jogs over, breathless. "You made it. Cool."

"Yeah, great game."

We stand there looking at each other, the zingy thing swirling between us through the little puffy clouds of our breath. Becky shifts her weight next to me, and I remember that my friends are waiting. And listening to every word.

Jesse clears his throat. "So—"

"Yo! Sanders! Get a move on!" Michael Deegan is so not my favorite person right now.

"So will I see you—" Jesse begins.

"Sanders! Seriously!"

Jesse shrugs sheepishly. "Later," he says with a wave. I'm not sure if it's a question or a statement. He runs back to his friends and the zingy thing travels away with him.

Then I see it. Jesse tangled in a knot of arms, a tribe of people so tightly knit that they look like one multi-limbed organism. A giant squid of humanity. Worst of all: the arm snaked around his waist belongs to Marlene James.

"Do you see what I see?" Monique says. Her hip is cocked in protest, a sneer on her lips.

"See what?" Sarah replies.

"That heinous she-creature has her talons all over Jesse."

"No," Sarah says, straining to get a closer look.

"Forget it, you guys," I say. "Let's just go."

A horn honks and Mrs. Dupree's SUV comes into view. Monique opens the door and we climb in. The cabin is too bright and garish. I just want to sit in the dark without everyone searching my face for clues about how awful I feel. There's no need to discuss the nauseous disappointment that's clawing at my insides.

Or the voice that's screaming in my head: *you do not belong with him. And you never freaking will.*

chapter nine

In the few delicious moments before the first light of morning, I am the Sugarplum Fairy. I wear a glittery pink tutu and a tiara with dangling teardrops. I spin delicately and balance en pointe for long, blissful moments.

"Indigo."

Yes, that's me.

"INDIGO!"

Oh. This isn't the dream anymore. Charlie stands by the side of my bed, his face etched with worry.

"What time is it?" I look at my clock. 7:43 am. How did I manage to sleep this late…and why did Mom let me?

"Mom's gone."

"She's not gone. She's probably just doing errands."

"No. *She's gone.* She left a note." He hands me a crinkled sheet of paper.

The note reads:

Dear Family,

I'm leaving. I am angry and tired all the time and I can't keep living this way. I don't expect you to understand. Forgive me.

Love,

Mom

Charlie's eyes fill with tears. "I'm scared, Indy."

My stomach twists. "It'll be all right." I pat his shoulder. "Let's go find her." I crumple the note in my fist.

I throw on warm clothes and my furry boots. I grab a protein bar and stick it in my coat pocket.

Where could she be? *Think, Indigo, think.* I look helplessly at the pile of mail in her "office" for clues, and an idea springs to mind. I think I know where to find her.

My hands shake a little as I pull on my gloves. I am freaked out and totally pissed at her. Even though she's a nightmare to live with, she can't just leave.

We grab our bikes and start riding. The early morning sky is an oppressive leaden grey. Bitter cold burns the ends of my fingers in the chilly wind.

"Where are we going?" Charlie calls into the wind.

"Just a little bit further," I yell back.

"Wait up!" While I stop to let Charlie catch up, I cup my hands together and blow on them to warm them up. They feel like they are permanently stuck in a handlebar-gripping position.

Charlie's lips look a little bit blue from the cold. "We'll slow down," I tell him, hoping we don't freeze before we get there.

The parking lot is deserted when we get there. It usually is during the off-season. Mom's car is parked down at the far end near the boat docks. The wooden gangplank that leads toward the beach is wet with morning dew; the carpet runner squishes underfoot with each step. I spot her on the far end of the beach and march ahead angrily. *Squish, squish, squish, squish.* My breath comes out in steamy puffs of smoke.

We find her huddled under a blanket, her face hidden under her wide-brimmed straw hat, the one she wears when she's gardening. She's reading a newspaper. *A newspaper.* Like she's on freaking vacation instead of ruining multiple lives at home.

She looks up at me, a blank expression on her face. I feel like shaking her. "Mom! How could you just leave like that? What is wrong with you?"

She looks down at her hands and seems surprised to see that they are holding a newspaper. She sighs heavily. "You don't know what it's like." Her voice is small and breathy, like she barely has enough power to get the words out. She finally looks at me. "I'm so tired. I never get a break. You don't understand."

I stare at her in disbelief. "You can't run off because you don't feel like being a Mom today."

Charlie starts crying. His tears mix with the snot dribbling out of his nose.

"Look at him, Mom. He needs you. You're not being fair."

She looks over at him, and her shoulders sag. "You're right," she says quietly. "But it's too much for one person. Where am I supposed to get help? Your father?" She snorts. "You? You're busy with your life and you can't wait to leave, anyway. So then what?"

"I don't know. Try talking to Dad. Or your friends. Maybe you could carpool or something. But you can't just leave."

"Mommy, don't leave," Charlie wails, his whole body shaking with sobs.

She holds out her arms to him and he sinks in her lap. She pulls the blanket around both of them and closes her eyes as she rocks him. "It's all right," she says, over and over. At last he stops crying and hugs her. She looks out at the ocean one last time and takes a deep breath, letting out a huge sigh. "Let's go home."

We carry her stuff to the car and throw our bikes in the back. We are all silent on the drive home. I turn up the heat and stuff my hands in my pocket. I feel the protein bar in there but there's no way I can eat it. Instead, I wonder if my mother is sane. Will she fall apart?

I can't let that happen – to any of us. I have to come up with a plan to keep her from losing it completely.

After dinner, Mom heads to the family room with a drink and a romance novel. I flip through the latest issue of "Dance" magazine. Brad puts on his headphones and zones out. The house is completely silent aside from the occasional clink of ice as Mom guzzles the drink that's balanced precariously in her lap while she reads.

She seems normal after this morning's drama. She may be over it, but I'm not. I can't concentrate; I keep sneaking looks at her.

Gradually her eyes close and her head nods forward. The book slides out of her lap. Brad looks over at me and silently points at her. His smirk says he finds it amusing. I shrug nonchalantly and sigh.

A few minutes later Mom pops back up like she's been cattle-prodded. She looks around. "Oh, well, will you look at that?" She smiles blankly.

Brad and I share a look. "Look at what?" Brad says.

"Can't you see the spirits? Right there on the TV." Her voice is sluggish.

"Mom, the TV is off," Brad says. He widens his eyes at me and silently mouths "WTF?"

"Mom, you were sleeping. It was a dream," I tell her.

She shakes her head loosely. "Silly Indy." She sounds like she's four years old. "They're still there. I can see them."

The hairs on my arms prickle strangely. I feel cold. Brad's brow furrows in anger and something else I can't quite read. "Mom. It's late. You should go to bed." He stands hastily and drags her by the elbow. Her slippers scuff noisily down the hall.

The empty family room buzzes with the echo of whatever weird thing just happened. Since I'm the only one left, I turn off all the lights. As I turn each one off, the unsettling feeling that I've missed something intensifies.

A final click and I'm alone in the dark.

chapter ten

Music pulses in my ears as I pump out leg lifts. I can't believe how much heavier my leg feels with the three-pound weight wrapped around my ankle. Miss Roberta swears these exercises build strength quickly. Tonight I've doubled up my reps; I need to keep my mind on something beside my problems.

I switch songs, choosing one that has a beat that drives me to keep going. I sing along quietly, allowing the lyrics to take my mind off the manic chaos that is now the new normal in my life. Mom was so bizarre earlier when Brad dragged her off to bed and no one else seems to notice or worry about it except me.

Ever since Miss Roberta told me I was still floppy in my middle I force myself to do extra ab work. Every abdominal exercise I can think of: crunches, roll-ups, static holds, bicycles. Tonight I channel all of my anxiety into making my belly stronger.

It's brutal and I hate it. When I'm done I collapse on my mat. I open my eyes and Brad's feet come into focus. He gestures for me to take off my headphones.

"We need to talk."

"Okay." I sit up.

"Why is Mom acting so psycho? And what the heck was that crap about spirits in the TV?"

I sigh. "I heard her telling Mrs. Rusch that she's dying."

"She gave me that same crap story the other day. When I nailed her with questions she had no answers. No name of her doctor. No lab results. Nothing. She's not dying." He pounds his thigh with his fist.

Pictures start to flash through my mind. I think about the mood swings. The rages. The weird nighttime dramas. I stare at my lap, thoughts racing. The pieces click into place, one after the other. The world starts to spin around me like a carnival ride.

Maybe it's something else.

"Indy?" Brad says quietly.

I look over at him, and then I know.

There's been a drink in her hand every single time.

I open my laptop. A search for the word "alcoholic" yields more than 71,000,000 hits. Okay. Obviously there are a lot of people out there with this problem. I click on the link for Alcoholics Anonymous. They gave a lecture at school last year about teen drinking. At the time it pretty much went straight over my head because I didn't know anyone with alcohol problems.

Until now.

I read that alcoholism is incurable. The only way to get over it is to stop drinking completely. Apparently women are more susceptible to becoming alcoholics than men.

And then I see it. The equation to pinpoint unhealthy alcohol use: *"How many times in the past year have you had X or more drinks in a day?" (where X is 5 for men and 4 for women).*

Finally. A real-life example where I can put algebra to use.

But a final question remains: if x (my mother, the wild card, the variable in this equation) won't stop drinking, then what?

Brad slips away and I read until my eyes get tired and my head starts to ache. Words swim through my brain. Addiction. Disease. Enabling. Denial. These are not words I want to own. Saying them leaves the tangy taste of metal in my mouth. But I know all about denial. It's been my go-to tactic for a long time. I haven't wanted to admit how much of a problem Mom's drinking has become. It's overwhelming. Rehabilitation, treatment centers and support groups, Al-Anon, Al-Ateen, AA, the whole family of twelve-steppers. It sounds like a dance people do in dimly lit bars wearing cowboy boots. The one dance I do not want to do.

My computer slips into sleep mode and the screen goes dark. I should probably do the same, but I can't. I can only sit here feeling empty while a thousand clamoring voices fight for space in my head. I can no longer talk myself out of facing this problem and what it means for all of us.

It's times like this when I feel like I need comforting from my mother.

But this time, she's the problem.

chapter eleven

A crescendo of violins and joyful chorus means only one thing in my house: Dad finally got the Christmas tree. Every year about two weeks before Christmas, Dad's internal alarm goes off and he goes into full-blown holiday mode. First comes the opera music, cranked up full blast. Then he yanks all the boxes of lights and ornaments out of the attic. He's probably already spent the entire morning unraveling and testing the strands of lights and replacing burnt-out bulbs. He can't stand to have one single non-functional light.

The living room is empty of human life but the tree is up in its usual corner, the blue velvet armchairs pushed aside to make room for it. The unadorned limbs tell me that Dad obviously started only a short while ago. Just beyond the tree, my brothers are the picture of holiday activity.

"We're settin' up the lights," Charlie tells me proudly from his spot on the floor. "I'm helping."

Dad and Brad bend their heads in concentration as they examine the strands of lights laid out on the floor. More coils of giant-bulbed outdoor lights lay stacked up by the front door.

"Yeah, he's been a whole lot of 'help' this morning," Brad says, scowling. "Why don't you guys start on ornaments? That would be the biggest help of all." He gives me a pleading look.

"Start with the non-breakable ones," Dad suggests.

I love unwrapping the ornaments. No matter how many times I've seen them all before, I still get a little secret thrill when I unwrap them, especially my favorites. There are the two little pearl-edged dioramas with gold, glittery trumpeting angels inside, silver chimes with eight metal reindeer, and the rainbow-feathered birds with their funny wire feet. Dad is the only one who can ever make them stand upright once they're attached to the tree.

Charlie and I find the box marked "non-breakable" and get to work. I grab a box of ornament hooks. We unwrap them one by one, attach an ornament hook, then lay them out on the couch. Mom floats by with a stack of paperback books tucked under her arm. She tiptoes through the Christmas-light obstacle course, angling them away from Dad, which can only mean one thing: she just got a new shipment of romance novels.

"Carry on, people, you're doing a fantastic job," she says. Apparently she has no intention of helping.

Brad and I shrug at each other while Dad remains oblivious. It's virtually impossible to break his concentration once he dives into tinkering with lights.

A part of me is relieved to not have Mom involved. Last year she totally lost it when two of her vintage ornaments were smashed – and one of them was so not Charlie's fault. Thor wagged enthusiastically about something and his tail sent it crashing to the floor.

Dad finishes hanging the lights and plugs them in. The tree looks instantly festive; the twinkle of rainbow colors casts a soft glow on the wall.

The three of us work mostly without speaking, just music filling the space between us. Listening to music while making something beautiful always leaves me feeling fulfilled and at peace. I hang another one of my all-time favorites – a glass dragonfly – and something relaxes in my bones. It's only now that I realize what I really want for Christmas: this.

I work through my warm-up, improvising with a lunch table instead of a ballet barre. I try not to gag on the permanent smell of pine fresh cleaner and old food.

The cafeteria does not work as a green room. Repulsive smells aside, it's also freezing in here.

A warm hand on my shoulder makes me shiver involuntarily.

"Just about show time," Becky says. She's wearing a body-hugging red velvet dress with a delicate feather trim.

"Wow. You look festive...and suggestive," I say with a nod of approval.

"Thanks. Can't sit down though. I might sit in something nasty by mistake."

I snort. "Tell me about it. Whoever had the brilliant idea of this being the green room should be publicly flayed."

"It's green in places." She wrinkles her nose. "Especially the corners." She leans in close. "So... anyone *special* coming tonight?"

"That would be a negative," I reply. "But then I didn't get a memo or anything."

Her face looks grim. "I'm sorry. I thought he'd say something to you."

"Doesn't matter. I'm over it. I've got other things on my mind."

"I get it." She sighs. "Well, anyways, I wanted to give this to you before you go on tonight." She hands me a small silver box topped with curlicue red and gold ribbons. "Go on – open it," she says, bouncing on her heels.

"You have to give me wrapping lessons," I tell her.

"I always mangle the ribbon with the scissors."

Inside there's a flower-shaped rhinestone hair comb with a cascade of sparkles and feathers. I turn the comb over in my hands, admiring the details. All those tiny stones. "It's beautiful. Where did you find it?"

"Oh, you know me. I'm always on the lookout. Found it at one of my thrift hotspots. It's vintage, too. Probably belonged to someone's grandma." She holds out a hand. "Here. Let me help you put it on."

I feel the teeth slide against my scalp as she maneuvers the comb under my bun.

She steps back to admire me. "Perfect." She fumbles in her purse for a second and pulls out a small compact. "Here, see for yourself."

I contort until I catch a glimpse of myself in the tiny mirror. The stones wink in the overhead light, and the feathers curve along the contour of my head. "Thank you," I say, giving her a hug. "You made my night."

Later, I stand onstage in the dark waiting for the music to start. The whole school is here, but there's no sign of Jesse and my parents never come to school functions. For just a moment I wonder who I'm dancing for and why I let Mr. L. talk me into this.

The light comes up and the first few notes sing to

me. I answer with my body. Pain and longing become jumps and turns. I reach my fingers and toes to the sky like I'm imploring someone up there to help. With each step I have a way to say the things I can't put into words.

When the audience claps, I walk forward to center stage to take my bow. I curtsy deeply and feel warmth in my muscles and my heart. Mr. L. smiles up at me and I smile back, glad he talked me into performing tonight. My eyes sweep the crowd, looking for Becky but she isn't sitting close enough for me to spot her. As the applause dies down, one person stands out, clapping slowly and louder than anyone else.

Marlene James is sitting a few rows back. She draws out her applause, a twisted sneer on her face. When she sees she has my attention, she innocently bats her eyes, smiles and tilts her head toward the person next to her. She puts her arm around Jesse's neck and pulls him close to whisper something in his ear. Then she languidly angles her head my way and winks.

And that's when the stage goes dark.

chapter twelve

"How could we have been so clueless?" Brad says.

"She's good at hiding it."

Brad shakes his head. "The breakfast of champions: orange juice and a shot of vodka." He snorts. "Unfreaking believable."

"I know." I leaf through the stack of pages I printed from the internet.

It feels strange to be holding our clandestine meeting in a room full of board games and Barbies, but the attic playroom is the most private spot in the house. No one ever comes up here anymore because it's haunted. Even now I feel like I'm being watched, but that could just be my paranoid streak.

"What do you think this place was used for back in

the day?" I ask. The murals on the ceiling feature ladies wearing jewel-toned gowns frolicking through the woods.

"Never mind that," Brad says darkly. "Check this out. Silver Hills treatment center is ten minutes from here."

"That could work. Now how do we tell Dad?"

"We're just going to lay out all the facts."

"I hope you're right."

"Don't freak out on me, Indy. It'll be fine."

"Fine is half-assed. We need better than fine."

We find our father in his office, putting stamps on a pile of mail.

"How about a walk, Dad?" I attempt to be casual. "Brad and I are going to the beach." I cross my fingers behind my back like I'm five again.

He stretches his arms overhead and yawns broadly. "Sure, guys. I need some fresh air." Brad and I give each other a silent thumbs-up behind his back.

The short walk to the beach takes forever because Thor stops to pee every three seconds. The ocean looks black under the marbled grey, but glaringly bright sky today; every ripple reflects a sparkle of light. Together they shine like a million tiny diamonds. It feels like a sign.

Brad breaks the silence. "Fresh air feels awesome. It's a relief."

"A relief?" Dad looks confused. "From what?"

"Mom's been wacko lately."

"She's under a lot of pressure. Taking care of you guys isn't easy," he says, smiling.

"She's been freaking out all the time. You should hear her."

"I've heard her."

"Dad." My throat feels tight. "Mom is an alcoholic."

"She has a stash of vodka six bottles deep, Dad," Brad adds.

Dad frowns at this. "You know we keep alcohol in the house. Your mom likes a cocktail in the evening. Heck, *I* like a cocktail in the evening."

Now I know he doesn't believe us. He doesn't want to. He'd rather pretend it all away.

"But Dad—" My voice sounds harsh and desperate. "This is serious!"

"Look," he says. "Your mother gets tired. That's all. She's under a lot of stress. He puts one arm around each of our shoulders. "She needs your help. So give her a break." The set of his jaw indicates that he's done discussing it.

Which is very bad news for us.

I whip off two turns, using my reflection in the mirror to spot. My landing is off. I try again. Still off. I don't know why. After our failed talk with Dad I came here to practice but it's making me feel worse.

"Anchor the supporting shoulder. It's throwing off your turns." Miss Roberta offers this comment without once taking her eyes off the newspaper. Apparently we can add x-ray vision to her list of superpowers.

I prepare again, this time focusing on my supporting side. I turn twice effortlessly and my body spins into a third rotation.

"Good. Do it again. At least three more times to be sure it sticks."

I do as she says. The turns are all fluid, the landings solid. If only it were that easy to fix my other problems.

"Ridiculous," she says.

I look at her. She's talking about something in the paper. Not my technique, thank God.

"Listen to this," she says, scowling. "Monique Dupree steals the spotlight with her sparkling presence. She is going places." She looks at me without blinking.

I'm not going to say anything bad about my friend and I'm not about to cross Miss Roberta either, so I opt for silence.

"Virginia Johnson has no idea what she is talking about. She doesn't even mention you, the most talented dancer in my school." She shakes her head. "Ridiculous," she says again.

Outside the studio window, the wind rushes through the trees, making their grey branches shudder. I run through my variation. Twice. The longer I stay here the less time I have to be at home.

I hit an arabesque. The music is sweet and light, a flute, like the sounds of birds in spring. But I am not a light, flitting bird. More like an ostrich. A heavy, flightless bird stuck on Earth.

During the waltz sequence, my favorite part of the variation, breath and movement synchronize and the rest of the world falls away. I will myself to finish the final turning sequence even though my body is trembling from exertion. Count, breathe, execute. I nail my final landing and the room goes silent.

I brush away rivulets of sweat around my hairline and brace my hands on my knees. I hear my breath coming out in ragged spurts.

"That's looking better." Miss Roberta's voice cuts through the quietness. She folds the paper and sets it aside, then looks at me. "You really caught hold of a driving force there. Would you say that's true?"

If she only knew the half of it.

I nod mutely and look at the floor.

"Well, whatever it is you're channeling, keep it up. It's working. When life throws things your way, use them to fly." She looks at the clock. "How did it get to be after six already?" She tosses the paper into her bag and shuts off the stereo. "I have to get going or I'll be late."

I pull on my yoga pants and a sweater over my sweaty dance clothes. Miss Roberta turns off the studio lights and we scurry down the stairs.

She laughs. "When we wear boots on these stairs, we sound like a herd of goats." Once we are outside she locks the front door and turns to me. "I'm having dinner with an old friend from New York."

"That's great," I say. Ever since her husband died suddenly two years ago, Miss Roberta has been a total recluse. I worry about her.

"I intend to ask her advice." She looks serious. "We have to be careful, Indigo. If I take you to New York too soon – before you are really ready – it could ruin your chances. I am going to ask her to observe class."

Her gloved hand touches my shoulder and gives it a squeeze. I know she is on my side, but it doesn't matter.

"All right, then." Her look says so much more. That she understands. That perhaps she has been there herself. That she wishes the best for me.

As I watch her tiny figure walk away under the distant beam of a streetlight, I realize it isn't enough.

chapter thirteen

It's so cold in the studio this morning that I can barely feel my toes, even though I've piled on every piece of warm up clothing I own: leg warmers layered on top of wool tights – on top of my leotard and regular tights. I've even got on a sweater and wrist warmers.

"Warm-up clothes are fine for the barre, girls, but it all comes off once we get to the floor. I need to see your lines clearly." There's a collective groan at this rule of Miss Roberta's. She's always adamant about this, regardless of the season.

My muscles feel brittle, like they're made of plastic. When I bend forward for the combré I'm so tight from the cold that touching my head to my shins is impossible.

Once we are out on the floor, I push myself to go faster, do more turns, imagining I'm already in New York. But then Miss Roberta shows a fouetté combination. Every dancer has their strengths and their Achilles heel. For some, it's the quick, tiny footwork of allegro jumps. For others, it's the adagio, which requires incredible strength and flexibility. For me, it's the fouetté.

The word fouetté means, "to whip." A dancer turns on one leg while whipping the other leg out to the side, then in and around. I am whipped by the thing that means, "to whip." I watch the other girls in the group and grit my teeth. Marlene is a fouetté machine. The girl was made to do fouettés. She does them perfectly, effortlessly, her face serene as she turns. For a minute, I hate her.

I know I am working myself into a frenzy and it's not even my turn. I have to stop psyching myself out. But how do I become one with the fouetté? I sneak another look at Marlene for clues.

When it's my turn, my legs go stiff with anxiety. My inner critic goes into overdrive and I can't concentrate. I look at myself in the mirror and start with a double turn, whipping my leg out. But I'm not on center. By the time I feel how off I am it's too late. My momentum is too strong. And then I'm airborne. Time takes on a strangely elastic quality. My arms windmill wildly. In that brief millisecond I know that I am falling. And it will hurt.

I crash to the floor. Pain radiates all through my left hip while bodies continue to fouetté around me. No one stops or looks at me. Class goes on; it has to. Even when dancers fall, the show must always go on.

I fight back tears. It's not just the turns. It's everything added together. I feel whipped in every way. Everything feels out of reach: New York, my dreams, my life. The ballet studio is supposed to be the one good part of my life, my sanctuary. My throat is tight and hot as emotions churn inside me.

Can't cry. Mustn't cry. I pull myself off the floor and hobble to the side of the room. I pull in ragged breaths, trying to calm myself down. The tears come, leaving warm salty tracks on my cheeks as they slide down to my chin and drop to the floor.

I make a beeline for the bathroom before anyone sees me crying. I hate myself for being so weak. I stare at my red, swollen face in the bathroom mirror. What is wrong with me? *Losing it over fouettés, how pathetic is that?* I stare at the mirror again, telling myself to pull it together and stop being a baby.

I can't stand looking at my reflection anymore so I sit on the toilet. I consider slapping some sense into myself but that probably won't help. I close my eyes and listen to my breaths. My shallow breathing, the air flowing in and out, sounds like ocean waves. When I can breathe normally again I splash cold water on my face and drink a few sips from my cupped hands.

When I reenter the studio, they've moved on to

jumps. Miss Roberta gives me a sidelong glance before yelling corrections at the others. "Assemblé, Michelle! It means to assemble! Tightly together! Suck it up, girls!"

I slip back into the group. I can't give up. I won't give up.

Fouettés are the least of my problems.

Whirr. Grind. Hiss. The background noise in Kubler's coffee shop reverberates in my skull. Every table is full. The overhead spotlights are too bright. There are a million people in here, all talking at once. I shift in my seat; the metal chairs are uncomfortably steely. Why did I let Monique talk me into coming? I'm only halfway here, anyway. I watch my friends chatting away and wonder how they remain oblivious to the obnoxious machinery churning out our caffeine highs.

Our table is repulsively sticky.

"Order up for Ashley!" The barista's voice jars me back into the moment. She starts foaming the next latté. The sound of steam hitting cold milk sounds like a large mammal trying to hock up a hairball.

"Right, but then what would you do? Go for it?" Monique's voice pierces through my cloud of disturbance. I have no idea what she's talking about.

Becky murmurs a response. Sarah nods, her eyes

still downcast in her lap.

My head aches and even though it's four o'clock, my brain is still fuzzy, like it's stuffed with cotton. Or maybe I'm already insane from too much thinking. I prop my chin on my hand, attempting to stay awake.

"Who's in for tomorrow night?" Becky says.

"In," Sarah says, still tapping out texts.

Monique shakes her head. "I've got dress rehearsal. It'll probably be a late night. Plus, I need my beauty rest."

Stress and worry wash over me in a giant wave. Part of me wants to spew about stuff at home but I don't think my friends can understand or help.

I can't do it alone. No one can. It's a crystal clear realization.

I take a deep, shuddery breath. I can do this. They are my friends. I have to say something. "Guys, I—"

Sarah snorts loudly. "Holy…guys…you have to see this!" She holds her phone up triumphantly. The others bend their heads to look.

And then I know. They can't possibly help me. What would they do anyway? Text my mother to death? I slouch in defeat.

"Earth to Indigo." Monique is staring at me, her eyebrows crimped together in a scowl.

"What? Sorry. Did I miss something?" I mumble.

"Jesus. What is with you lately?" Her mouth is a grim line. "And you," she says, glaring at Sarah. "Put that thing away. Don't you know it's rude to text at the table?"

Sarah stares at her open-mouthed for a second before tossing the phone in her purse.

Monique continues. "Anyway. Who's coming on Saturday?"

"Saturday?" I ask.

"Do not tell me you forgot. The show, Indigo. My show, the one I've been rehearsing for three months?" she sputters. "Please tell me you know what I'm talking about."

"I—" I fumble. Brain not working.

"Dammit, Indy. This is the most important thing I've done like, ever. It's a big deal. For me. But apparently not for you."

"Look, M, I'm sorry. I'm just tired. I can't even think straight right now. I just spaced."

"Well, guess what? I'm tired, too. Tired of being treated like I'm not important."

The air rings with the harsh tone of her words. She's got it all wrong, of course. She matters more than she knows. But she doesn't know that I feel like I'm drowning. And now is not the time to tell her.

I don't have the energy for a fight or a witty comeback, so I take the coward's way out. "You're right. I'm sorry. You know what, I'm gonna go. I need some sleep."

I grab my stuff, giving them a wan smile before I take off. Just before I walk out the door, the coffee grinder goes off again and I jolt. Every nerve in my body is fried. Is this what it feels like to hit rock bottom?

A cloud of steam billows out through the doorway as I make my escape. Even the wisps of smoke are more substantial than I am right now.

chapter fourteen

My phone makes an angry chattering noise as it vibrates across the desk. I open my eyes slowly and curse the caller for waking me up this early. Muted, silvery light fills the room. Outside my window the world is still and white. It looks new under a uniform blanket of snow, treetops look like they've been coated in whipped cream. Magic happened while I slept.

I'm surprised to see Monique's number on the screen. I almost don't answer it, but morbid curiosity wins out.

"Yes?" My voice is crisp and business-like. I'm still upset with her, even after a full night's sleep.

"Indy, I need your help."

I snort. "Why don't you call one of your more

attentive friends?"

"Last night I slipped and twisted my ankle, Indy. It's sprained. There's no way I can do the show. Please. I need you. You're the only one who can learn it in time." Her voice wavers with sadness. This show was supposed to be her first real solo and her debut as a choreographer. I feel a slight thaw coming on.

"Geez, M, why'd you have to go and do a silly thing like that?"

"I know, right?" Her tears mix with laughter. "Will you do it?" she whispers.

"You know, I have a very busy performing schedule this month," I say. I have to make her squirm a little. "But I suppose I could squeeze you in."

"I knew it! You'd better get over here right away. Dress rehearsal is tonight!"

"Fine, but it's going to cost you a big, fat latté. With perfectly foamed milk, or I walk."

I scribble a quick note detailing my excuse for exiting the ongoing Shakespearean tragedy that is my home life. Once outside, the cold burns my cheeks and nose and tickles the inside of my nasal passages. I feel like I might sneeze.

Everything is silent as I tramp down the block admiring the frosted landscape. Trees droop under the weight of the snow and the road has not been plowed. Sky, ground, and everything in between is white and peaceful.

I don't get a chance to knock on the front door

before Monique jerks it open and pulls me inside. "Hurry up. You've got a lot to learn," she says, giving me a quick hug. Whatever weirdness there was between us yesterday dissolves in the middle of the embrace.

"Whoa, sister, we had a deal, remember? If I'm going to stuff my head with a bunch of choreography this early in the morning, I need a healthy dose of caffeine first."

True to her word, she brews me up a mean latté. The girl has foaming perfected to a science.

I slip on my ballet slippers and we get to work.

We start by walking through the steps several times so I can learn the staging before I perfect the choreography. Hours tick by as she hobbles around her living room, showing me her part. It's not a simple part, either. Translating it from the living room to the stage is going to be difficult.

Monique counts each beat out loud, slowly. Gradually, it starts to sink in. But learning choreography in the living room while trying not to trip over the furniture is starting to wear on me.

As if on cue, Monique's mom wanders in with a plate of cookies. "I thought you could use some sustenance," she says. She leaves with a smile.

A few cookies later we do a final run-through, just to be sure. Monique's dog, Tilly, a fluffy white Maltese, lies on the couch, sleeping.

I envy her.

"I think you've got it," Monique says.

I exhale with relief and look at the clock. We've got two hours until dress rehearsal.

"Now for the partnering section."

"P-partnering section?" I sputter. I've never danced with a guy before. "I can't—I've never—" *Breathe, Indigo, breathe.* "Who is it?" And where is this partner, anyway?

"Austin McCarthy. Do you know him?"

"He's only the hottest guy on the gymnastics team! Oh God, this can't be happening to me. I can't even look the guy in the face and now we're supposed to be all up in there with each other?"

"He's a great partner and he's super strong."

I am doing the breath of panic. I will never survive this.

"And stop doing the breath of panic. You'll be fine."

"Assuming I actually survive, when am I supposed to rehearse with this guy?"

"I told him to come to the theater a little early so you guys can practice."

"A little early? How early?"

"Half an hour."

"That's not enough, M! I need more time just to find the courage to look him in the face!"

Thirty minutes is not enough time to get through security lines at the airport. It certainly isn't enough time to get over major nerves while one of the hottest guys in school lifts you into his arms.

Austin shows up late. He smiles and I can't breathe, thanks to the hot guy's tardiness and my own utter lack of confidence. Plus we have to rehearse in the lobby because the chorus is using the stage.

I should never have agreed to do this. I could be home drinking hot cocoa right now, but no, I had to be a hero.

"Are you ready?" he says.

"Sure." I look at his hands. Hands that will soon be all over my body.

"All right, guys," Monique says, taking charge. "The first lift is a simple fish dive. Indy, you'll strike into an arabesque, then Austin will lift you. Let's try it once."

Austin's blue eyes are fixed on me as I move into the position. I feel like I might melt into a puddle at the guy's feet. I hit the arabesque and feel his hands on my waist and thigh. He lifts me, and struggles. Is it possible he's as nervous as I am?

"Come back up and release her."

He sets me down and relief floods my body.

"Good." Monique folds her arms and nods approvingly. "Now for the last piece. The catch after the grand jetés."

We practice a few times before we realize we

should already be backstage. We grab our bags and run through the stage door, Monique hobbling behind us.

"See ya onstage," Austin says. He disappears into the men's dressing room. Monique leads me into the women's.

All heads turn as we enter. Everyone looks friendly except for Virginia Johnson, no big surprise. Mirrors framed by bright bulbs run along the front wall. The performers all sit at makeup-littered tables; it looks like a bomb went off at Sephora.

After brief introductions to everyone, Monique points to an empty chair. "This is us, right next to Jerry. I'll make a little room for you." She sweeps her makeup aside. "You get ready and I'll find the costume."

Jerry asks a million questions while I work on my makeup. I answer her vaguely. She's very friendly but I need some peace before I go onstage.

Monique comes in holding a costume. It's a hideous shade of green with torn edges and a perky little apron in front.

"Please tell me that's not for me," I say.

"It looks like it's for a kindergartener, doesn't it?" She hands it to me.

"So much for wooing the hot gym guy's heart." I slip it on. I try an arabesque and frown. "The skirt is way too tight. It needs to be fuller."

Backstage, my eyes adjust quickly in the dark. Other cast members are there rehearsing their lines; some sing, a few chat in the corner. I warm up on my own. I'm already so nervous I feel like I might implode.

"Walk it through with me one last time?" I beg Monique. Even though there's no audience today, dress rehearsal is one step away from a real performance and I've never tried this thing on stage. I feel cold even after my warm-up. My body trembles with nerves.

The stage is gigantic compared to Monique's living room. The house lights are still on so I see rows of empty seats instead of the mirrors I look at every day in the dance studio. I always find that so disorienting. Today I feel like I might fly off the edge of the stage.

"Where the hell is Austin?" I'm not sure if she says this or I just think it.

Austin arrives at last.

"Way to leave things to the last second," Monique mumbles.

Just as we are trying the first lift, the lights dim and the stage manager calls for us to take our places.

The theater goes black.

Familiar music pours through the speakers. My cue. I see Austin waiting in the wings on the other side of the stage. The moment I enter, I feel everyone watching me, waiting to see if I know what I'm doing. Adrenaline courses through my body. I feel strange and shaky, like my muscles aren't under my control, yet light and fluttery at the same time, like I could fly away.

The flute sings a fluttery melody and my feet move quickly. The confusing part is coming. I do a double turn, spotting a red light at the back of the theater. What comes next? Right. Eight counts of waltz step. Then what? My mind goes absolutely blank. This is the part I keep forgetting. I am standing here with no clue what comes next.

Seconds go by. I see wide eyes all around me; the rest of the cast now knows I. Have. No. Idea. What. I'm. Doing.

And then Austin is there. I strike the arabesque and feel his strong hands, not shaking this time. He lifts me and there is a giant tearing sound. The costume from hell rips wide open. My butt is totally exposed (except for the minimal coverage one gets from a pair of pink tights). As everyone knows, ballet dancers always go commando. There's no time to stop. The finale music is thunderous. I channel my anger into flying through the air before Austin catches me. Only he doesn't.

Catch me, that is.

Instead we both go down, a tangled mass of limbs, confusion, and ugly costumes. I catch Virginia's knowing smirk just before the stage goes dark again.

I'm the first to return to the dressing room, where I tear off the costume. The stage door opens as I'm frantically shoving my tights in my dance bag.

"You doin' okay, kiddo?" Jerry asks, her face full

of compassion.

Monique hobbles in behind her. "Don't worry, Indy. You have this down, I know you do."

I hear Virginia's twangy voice. "I am just appalled. She calls herself a professional dancer. Who is she kidding? I mean, really!"

The other women around her titter in response, but fall silent when they see me standing there.

For a second I think Virginia is right. Who am I kidding? Then I remember that these Connecticut nobodies have no business judging me. Maybe I should remind them that without me, this show is down the tubes.

I've got this down. A few more practice runs onstage and I can do this.

But first I have to torch the frickin' costume.

That night, it's no big surprise that I can't fall asleep. The day's horrible suckitude plays over and over in my mind, no matter how hard I attempt to turn it off. I try reminding myself that an awful dress rehearsal is an omen for a great performance. Make all your mistakes before you have an audience.

It's a nice theory but right now it isn't working.

I remember reading about this Olympic athlete who drove his coach crazy because he lay in his hammock and visualized winning while the other athletes were out there running around. The coach was tearing his hair out, but the technique totally worked. The guy won a bunch of gold medals and became famous.

So I decide to give it a try. Why not? It's not like things could get any worse. While swirling pictures continue to dance behind my eyelids, sleep finally comes like a blissful dusting of snow.

chapter fifteen

"They salvaged the costume!" Monique is ecstatic.

"This is not happy news in my world," I reply.

"It really is better, I promise."

"A *paper bag* would be better."

"Look, they added a panel to make the skirt fuller. Tearing it during dress rehearsal was the best thing that could have happened."

Easy for her to say, she didn't end up with her ass on display. In my opinion the best thing for the costume would be spontaneous combustion. But it's hard to be mad in the face of her twinkly attitude.

I finish my hair and makeup and pull on a sweatshirt and leg warmers and head backstage. There's no way I'm hanging around the hostile cave of the dressing room. I need time to warm up thoroughly and practice the lazy Olympian's technique. Grabbing Austin for a few more practice runs probably wouldn't be a bad idea, either.

It's cold and dark backstage, but I have it to myself. I stretch awhile and then sit with my back against the wall and close my eyes, playing my part in my head like a movie. My body relaxes as pictures flash behind my eyelids.

"Sleeping isn't part of the job description."

My eyes fly open. "What isn't part of the job description?"

Austin stands above me, looking superior. "Sleeping."

"I wasn't sleeping, I was practicing."

"Looked like sleeping to me."

"Whatever. As long as you're standing here, why don't we practice for real?"

When we rehearse, he stands so close that when he says, "Go for it," his breath caresses the back of my neck. Strangely enough, I realize I feel nothing. No chemistry, no buzz... I mean, here he is, one of the buffest guys at school, and I'm totally not into him. Interesting.

Once we get the catch down, I feel better. I go through my mental checklist: shoes on with no chance of coming off, a final spritz of hairspray. I keep moving so my muscles stay warm and I take deep breaths to calm the butterflies that come before every show.

Lights. Curtain.

I tell myself that today's show will be amazing. I almost believe it as I move into the wings for my first entrance. *Focus, Indigo. It's time to dazzle.* I look out into the sea of silhouettes in the dark theater before me and feel both exhilarated and slightly nauseous.

I give myself to the music. My limbs sing feelings into shapes. My heart pumps a rhythm; I live for this. I love it. Live. Love. I feel so powerful, I must be trailing a shower of sparks behind me.

If thunderous applause is any indication, we are a huge success. Did someone say "encore?"

There's a celebration afterward at Jonnie's Joint, the local caffeine hot spot. It's a hopping Saturday night, and we manage to snag a spot in the far corner near the fireplace. The brown pleather couch was past its prime two or three owners ago but I sink into it gratefully and let the post-show high work its wonders. Between that and the fireplace, my legs feel warm and gooey.

The fashion clones are out in droves, of course, since this is pretty much the only afterhours place for our crowd. Marlene James and her minions are perched on stools at the counter, sipping frothy drinks. They cackle like showy birds after every joke from their jock entourage. Like the world needs more Christmas voices. I roll my eyes and look away.

"Repulsive," Monique says, eyeing them.

"I know. I wish they'd shut it."

"How can they drink those things and stay thin? Each one of them has about a million calories. Did you see all of that whipped cream?"

"Being a jock has benefits," Austin quips. "You can eat whatever you want."

Monique elbows him in the side. "Not to be confused with being a *jerk*."

"I don't know anything about that. Anyway, I'm buying. I feel invincible tonight."

We give him our orders and watch him swagger off.

"Look at him," I say. "He's swaggering."

"Doesn't it look good?" Monique's eyes remain riveted on him.

He turns around and catches her staring. He smiles widely.

"Hold up. That penetrating gaze he just threw over this way was *not* directed at me." I grin at her. "Is there a little somethin', somethin' going on here?"

Monique turns pink and looks down at her lap.

"Oh my God, there *is* something! You're blushing!" I've never seen my friend's face turn this particular shade of crimson. "Spill it."

"There's definitely chemistry and we've spent a lot of time together rehearsing. So far it's been lingering looks, subtle stuff like that."

"That last look from him wasn't subtle," I say. "But then again, what do I know? I'm the last person to look to for dating advice."

"We'll see. Anyway, I'm a hopeless romantic. I want him to make the first move and sweep me off my feet."

"Well, that should be easy while you're gimping around."

Austin returns. "Lattés all around," he says, plopping down next to me. He leans back into the wrinkled couch, draping his arms along the back of it. His fingers trail near my shoulder.

"Get comfortable, why don't you," I say.

"I have. Believe me, I have." He closes his eyes for dramatic effect. He pops back up. "I almost forgot to tell you…you should have seen Virginia during your solo. She looked so mad I thought her pancake makeup was going to crack off."

"Nailing tonight's performance was cathartic, especially if it meant proving her wrong."

"Mean people suck!" Monique adds, and we bust up. Austin laughs so hard he's draped across my back.

I sit up and wipe away tears with my sleeve. I blink and Jesse comes into view, standing by the front door. No, scratch that. Frozen by the front door is more accurate. He stares at our cozy little group, and I can only imagine what he thinks. Austin's leg is pressed tightly against mine; his arm is still draped across me. It must look like we are comfortable together. After all, less than an hour ago Austin's hand was quite intimate with my inner thigh, though he'd much rather have his hand on Monique's thigh.

But Jesse doesn't know that.

His jaw tightens as he looks away. He stalks up to the counter and turns his back to us. Marlene James leans in for the kill. Her overdone laughter ratchets up an octave as she traces a finger along Jesse's shoulder.

My stomach drops to my feet. I sit there woodenly while Monique and Austin razz each other, fanning the flames of their budding romance. Of all the moments to run into Jesse, why in the cosmos did it have to be now?

The laughter and warmth in the room doesn't touch the chill running down my arms. Neither do the flames from the fireplace dancing along my left side. Every bit of post-performance radiance has been sucked away in seconds. Now I am only tired and worn, which is my cue to exit.

"Guys, I'm toast. I'm gonna take off."

Monique's mouth says, "Aw, are you sure?" But her eyes sparkle wickedly from the prospect of time alone with Austin. I don't blame her. It's not every day you get your storybook romantic moment.

Austin gives me a quick hug. "You were awesome tonight. I don't know how you pulled it off. You are going places, girl."

After he says this, I feel it: my future, waiting for

me in the wings. One step at a time, little by little, I will get there.

Outside, the sudden drop in temperature is a smack in the face. But the night is clear, full of more stars than usual, millions of twinkling miniature suns. I hear a little bell chiming somewhere off in the distance. It feels like a sign. Or maybe an angel just got their wings.

Icy snow crackles underfoot. I've got at least ten minutes to kill before Dad shows up, provided he actually left when I called him. A sudden movement makes me flinch, but it's only a cat. It meanders over for attention and I bend down to pet it. It's an odd-looking thing; both halves of its face are a competing mishmash of calico colors.

I laugh. "You can't make up your mind what color you are, can you?" I scratch it under the chin and it winds itself in and out of my legs. "Never mind, you're perfect the way you are...and awfully cute." I stand back up.

"I could say the same about you," says a familiar voice.

I see the slope of Jesse's shoulders under the streetlight. "What are you doing here?" I ask.

"After I grabbed a coffee I went over to say hello to you, but you'd already gone. I wanted to ask your friends where you were but they were busy. It's hard to dispense information when your lips are attached to someone else's." He grins. "Then I saw you through the window."

"Really…" I say, playing it casually. *I am so calling her first thing tomorrow to get the full details.*

I've also stopped breathing because he's standing here in front of me, all six-foot-whatever gloriousness of him.

Dad pulls up beside me and honks. Figures he'd be prompt *this* time.

"I've gotta go," I say.

I look at him and think about how I want his arms around me. I don't know whose rules are right anymore. Maybe it's time I make some of my own rules for a change.

I hug him and the zingy thing comes alive, zipping up my spine, even though I know Dad is a few feet away in the car.

And then, before I completely lose my nerve, I let go and get in the car. I can't look at Dad right now, so I look straight ahead while my heart pounds like galloping hooves. I shove my hands in my pockets and try not to shiver.

"Well," Dad says, "looks like you just made someone's night."

Jesse stands where I left him. Our eyes lock and he lifts a hand in a slight wave as we pull away. He stays there until I lose sight of him in the darkness.

chapter sixteen

Monique's room looks like an F4 tornado swept through it. Her lavender silk comforter has vanished under an unruly pile of dresses. A collection of shoes lies in a disorganized heap on the floor.

"Seriously. I don't want to do this," I moan.

Everyone brought stuff to try on and share and things are completely chaotic. Monique reappears from her closet with more dresses. "Yes you do," Monique says. "It'll be fun, and besides, Jesse asked you."

"He didn't *ask* me, he asked if I was *going*."

"He wants you there."

I sigh. "I hate trying on clothes."

Now I have not one, not two, but three wardrobe assistants helping me decide on the perfect outfit.

Although Sarah doesn't really count since she's been talking on her phone since she got here.

Monique pokes Sarah on the shoulder and says in an excessively sweet voice, "Who are you talking to?"

"Tommy." Sarah looks at her. "Why?"

Without answering, Monique wrestles the phone from Sarah's hands. "Hello, Tommy? Sarah has to go," she says. "We're in the middle of something. She'll call you back, K?"

"Why did you do that?" Sarah is indignant.

"Because your body is here but your brain is on planet Tommy. We need your opinion." She holds up two dresses for Sarah's inspection. "Becky says silver sparkles, I say black beaded. What do you think?"

Sarah glares at her. "I don't know. I think I need to see them on again."

"Like you even saw them the first time."

"Okay, okay, don't get your knickers in a knot. Put the first one on again, Indigo. I promise you have my full attention." She leans back on her elbows.

I put the silver one on again and sigh loudly. I'm tired and when I look at the pile of castoffs on the bed, I see why. I hope they pick the silver one so I can be done with this exercise.

Sarah narrows her eyes while she assesses. "No, not that one. Even though it sparkles, it doesn't make *you* sparkle. Am I right?" She asks, looking at the others. "I mean, it makes her look frumpy. Is it possible to be sparkly *and* frumpy?"

"I like this dress. Or at least I used to," I say, pulling it off. "Maybe I'll start a collection for our next clothes swap. Frumpy-sparkly is definitely not the look I'm after."

But now I have to put on the black beaded dress that's a total pain to get into. You have to sort of contort and slither into it while wrenching your head and one arm through the open side with the zipper. It's a Betsy Johnson I got on sale after I begged my mom to buy it for my birthday last year.

"Someone help me pull it over my shoulder, will you?" I say, wrestling my head through the hole. Becky tugs it down while I wiggle my hips. Finally we get it zipped up.

"That looks hot," Sarah says.

So it's decided.

Now I just have to learn to dance. The sad truth is this: I look like an electrocuted chicken when I try to move to pop music. Shaking my hips is completely foreign.

"I don't know, you guys. I don't think I'll ever get it."

"Nonsense." Sarah turns on some music. "Watch and learn," she says, cranking up the volume. Her second favorite hobby is watching music videos and learning the choreography. Before she got into soccer, she was the reigning hip-hop queen at her dance studio. "It's all in the hips. Here, try this." She grabs my hand and pulls me in front of the closet mirror. "Start out going side to side. Right. Okay, now do some hip circles with me."

Becky and Monique clap along for moral support.

"Keep going...now speed it up a little."

"My hips won't go any faster and I'm pretty sure I look like someone's cattle-prodding me," I say.

"Girlfriend, maybe you'd better just stick to slow dancing," Sarah says, laughing.

My phone rings in the eerie, alien sci-fi ring tone I've assigned to Mom because life with her is like living in *The Twilight Zone*. I roll my eyes and motion to the girls to turn the music off.

"I need to get going anyway," Sarah says. Which translates to: I need to call Tommy because it's been more than five minutes since I talked to him.

"You left the goddamn DVD player on again." Mom has this annoying habit of just diving right into conversations. No greeting, no pleasantries. Already looking for a fight.

She's not going to get one from me. "Gosh, Mom. Sorry about that."

"You also didn't collect the laundry like I told you to."

I roll my eyes at my friends as she continues listing every mistake I've made since the dawn of time.

"You hear me?"

"Yes, Mom. Got it."

"I don't like your tone, young lady. Do you really hear me or is this more lip service?" Mom says.

"Because I am tired of your attitude. You'd better get your butt home on time tonight, or I swear to God, ballet is off. I don't care what Miss Roberta says."

There's a click and she's gone. I squint my eyes shut and set the phone down on Monique's dresser with shaky hands. Mom's threats and attacks always come out of nowhere.

"What do you think, up do or down?" Becky asks, holding her hair on top of her head and sucking in her cheeks.

"What are you wearing, again?" Monique asks.

"Purple strapless."

I sit heavily on the chair in front of Monique's desk and ride out the post-Mom shockwave in silence.

"Up, for sure," Monique answers. "Oh, and I brought the vanity valise."

Also affectionately known as the Trollop Trunk, Monique's makeup kit is the biggest one I've ever seen, with something like three trays of eye shadow, lipsticks, blush, color corrector, and glitter. Monique has been the resident makeup artist for all of us since she got the kit for her birthday last year.

She puts some finishing touches on Becky's makeup. "Your eyes look amazing," she says, holding up a mirror. "They're like five times larger."

Becky grins. "At least something can compete with my chest for a change. That's what guys see first."

"Well, they are the first things to enter the room," Monique teases and Becky sticks her tongue out at her.

"You're up next, Indigo."

I close my eyes and let her work her magic. The makeup brushes are soft caresses as they sweep across my face. It's like having someone brush your hair, but better. The giant powder brush is the softest of all.

"Open." She's all business, with hawk-like focus as she works. "Look up." She sweeps mascara on my lashes. I struggle to keep my eyes open and they burn with the effort. She rests her pinkie on my cheek and draws on eyeliner, her patented technique for dramatic eyes. "Okay. Take a look."

"Wow," I say. "Thanks, M. I look—"

"Older? More glamorous?" She winks. "You're gonna knock him dead."

I wonder what it's like to have the confidence to wink at people. Winking is not my thing, but I'd love to borrow some of her attitude.

I look in the mirror again and see my smiling, happy friends. What more do I need?

It's dark inside school when we arrive. The music is so loud that it's traveling through the closed doors of the gym. The walls throb with the beat. Becky marches up to the doors. "Let's go have ourselves some fun," she says, yanking them open.

Giant star lights hang from the ceiling. Streamers

and balloons in white, blue and silver are scattered throughout the gym. There are a few couples dancing, but everyone else is divided into clusters. Most of the guys are over near the bleachers on the far side of the room. The "It" girls are standing by the punch bowl. Most of them are wearing the tiniest, tightest dresses they can get away with and their up-dos look vaguely similar. They must have had a group field trip to the Hair Company earlier today. Miriam and Missy, the twins who live down the road from me, walk in with boys I don't recognize. Probably guys from Gilman College, since the twins only date older guys.

I stand there uncertainly. Why does every party have to have this awkward moment where you stand there and people look at you and you wonder what to do and why you came? Or, in my case, if you should be here at all?

I swallow hard, trying to loosen the lump in my throat, but it doesn't help. Then I see Jesse. He's wearing some vintage jacket and his hair is spiked in front. He looks so good it's almost painful. He talks animatedly to his posse; they're all laughing. His eyes meet mine and I see other heads in his group swivel my way. The pack of them elbow each other in the sides. Michael Deegan grabs Jesse from behind in a neck lock and pulls him off his seat. Jesse's feet fly up as both of them land with a crash on the floor.

Boys.

"Let's go get some punch," Monique suggests. We

head over to the refreshment table, which is now free from posers. We grab drinks and stand in a little circle.

Becky stares at the ceiling. "I dig the stars," she says. "I want some of them for my room."

Sarah's head swivels back and forth between the soccer team (assembled in a pack by the DJ) and her phone.

"Will you put that thing away?" Monique hisses. "It's obnoxious to ignore the friends who are standing right in front of you." Sarah defiantly throws her phone in her purse with a scowl. "Am I wrong here?" Monique looks to us for backup.

Becky's eyes widen. "Jesse's headed this way."

And then he's standing here. "Good evening, ladies," he says. "Everyone looks stunning tonight."

I'm not sure if I imagine it or not, but my friends suddenly disappear. As in vanish...or maybe my eyes don't see anything except him. Does the music stop? I'm not sure, but I don't hear it anymore.

"You look great, Indigo."

"Thanks," I croak.

"Dance?" he asks, with a slight bow of his head.

I can't dance to this music. I'll look like an idiot and he will run away screaming. "M-maybe a little later," I stutter.

"Sure. How about a walk?"

"Okay." Walking I can do.

He gives me his elbow and pulls me close. As we walk toward the doors, I look over to see Monique and

Becky smiling at us. Becky gives me a thumbs-up before we exit the gym.

The hallways look different at night; it's strange to see them so empty, the rows of lockers like silent sentries. That zingy thing is in overdrive, making my legs quivery. The buzz of excitement pulses in my fingertips.

"Do you remember when we talked at the Labor Day party last summer?" He asks out of nowhere.

Do I remember? How could I forget? It all comes back with startling detail: Jesse beside me, our feet almost touching while we sat on lounge chairs, his skin golden in the end-of-day sunshine. We ate hot dogs and laughed about the beach groupies who seemed to live the entire summer on that tiny stretch of sand.

I laugh again at the memory. "That's the first time you ever talked to me."

"No it wasn't," he says. "You've forgotten all about Liz's party, then."

"Oh God, you're right!" I say, heat creeping into my face.

"I guess I made quite an impression." He laughs.

We look at each other, finally. His eyes are dark and serious. Could he be nervous, too? Are we all the same – worried about rejection? Okay, maybe not exactly the same, since he's a guy, but *still*.

He takes my hands, and I don't want him to ever let go. There are little pricks of starlight in his eyes. Or maybe it's just the reflections from the overhead lights. It doesn't matter because this is a perfect moment, the kind of moment you want to catch in your hands before it flies away. I feel like spinning through the hall.

He clears his throat. (He *is* nervous!) "I've wanted to know you better since then. But the right time kept slipping away." He tightens his grip on my hands. "Now feels right. What do you think?"

I nod my head mutely. "Come on," he says. "I think I hear a slow one."

I feel everyone's eyes on us when we return to the gym together. It's like being stalked in the forest by wild cats, their eyes glittering in the darkness while they salivate, thinking about the tasty meal ahead. *Let them salivate.* At least there are a few friendly grins out there to balance it all out. Monique gives me "the eye" and a coy little smirk, and Becky grins at me over her dance partner's shoulder.

Jesse holds me close while I rest my head on his shoulder and close my eyes as we spin under the stars. I want to save this feeling forever, press it between the heavy pages of my journal, the one with the buttery smooth blue leather cover. He is all warmth and certainty, and I am dancing on a cloud.

The song ends and the music abruptly shifts back to a throbbing beat. Just beyond Jesse's shoulder, the giant clock above the bleachers comes into view. I realize, with a start, how late it is. I have to leave – right now – or Mom will be livid. My life will be over for good.

Fear swirls up my throat. Stupid. So stupid. This is what happens when I forget, even for a second, that I'm not a normal person.

No matter what I'm trying to be tonight, I'm not a normal person. I'm a dancer. But not for long if I'm late.

"I have to go." *I have to get out of here. I shouldn't have come.* The crackle of anxiety urges me to push through clumps of sweaty bodies.

I find Becky and Monique near the door, laughing with a few of Sarah's soccer buddies.

"Can we go home?" I say, trying not to sound insane. "I feel like I might throw up." It isn't far from the truth.

Becky gives me a searching look. She nods slowly. "Sure. Let's go."

The kitchen is dark except for the faint glow of lights from the family room. Strange shadows lurk along the edge of the kitchen floor. The glowing blue numbers on the stove read 11:37 pm, digital proof that I'm home 37 minutes after curfew.

I have to turn off all the lights Mom left on without waking her up. It would be so easy if we didn't live in this old house with creaking bones, like some cranky old lady who can't wait to give away our secrets.

I tiptoe through the kitchen. Thor lifts his head for a moment as I pass his bed next to the refrigerator. He sighs and goes back to sleep. Some watchdog.

I sidestep the squeaky stair that leads to the family room and she's right there. Mom is asleep with her head on the table, inches away from a mostly eaten container of spaghetti. There's a thread of drool at the corner of her sauce smeared mouth. One arm is curled almost lovingly around the congealed food. The glass of melted ice near her hand holds the remains of her drink and the green glass ashtray beside her is filled with a collection of red-stained cigarette butts. I wonder wildly how many of them are stained with lipstick and how many with tomato sauce.

Disgust rears up like a kick to the gut. I swallow hard and turn away, quickly calculating how to tiptoe past her and leave her to deal with the mess when she wakes.

" 'S you," she says, her voice furry with sleep and drink. "Waa timezit?" She yawns, flakes of crusted tomato sauce rain from her lips. She looks at me blearily eyed.

I fight back the boiling urge to shake her or just walk out the back door and keep walking until I find some other sensible person to take me in. But I can't do any of those things.

"It's time to go to bed, Mom," I sigh.

chapter seventeen

"Girlfriend, are you actually *swooning*?" Monique's voice interrupts my thoughts as I stretch and mentally replay the magic moments with Jesse. She gives me the once over and says, "You *are* swooning! Someone should choreograph a new ballet for you— Swoon Lake. You can be the lead."

I glare at her and resume stretching. I am not in the mood to be hassled by anyone today. I'm so tired that it hurts. Between getting home late and then losing sleep over Mom, I can count the amount of hours I slept on one hand. Plus we are stuck in the tiny dressing room until the younger girls finish class and free up the studio. There are too many bodies crammed into this tight space. I angrily tug on my leg and wrench it into a stretch.

"Weren't you supporting the whole thing? That was you, wasn't it? Not someone who looks like you?" I say.

This earns me an exasperated sigh and an eye roll. "You know I am. I'm just joking."

"Ha ha."

"Speaking of hard times, how did it go when you got home last night? Did your mom freak?"

No, she passed out in a pan of spaghetti. "I snuck in. No prob."

"Lucky break."

That's one way of looking at it.

The divider to the studio slides open and we sidestep the rogue wave of young dancers pushing to get out. Their jostling knees and elbows are more than slightly annoying. They have no concept of spatial awareness.

I grab my place at the barre, guzzle a few sips of water. A woman I've never seen before is sitting in the window seat at the front of the classroom. She's blonde and slim, and although she's on the older side, everything about her says she's a dancer. She must be Miss Roberta's friend.

Freaking perfect.

I wipe sweat from my face and neck while we take a quick break to switch into our pointe shoes for variations at the end of class. I tie my ribbons slowly and carefully. My tired brain feels foggy; plus it keeps replaying little vignettes of Jesse.

"Are you still inhabiting this planet or are you visiting Swoon Lake again?" Monique whispers furtively. She widens her eyes, jerking her head toward the windows. I look over to find Miss Roberta staring at me intently.

If she notices my lack of focus I will never hear the end of it.

Miss Roberta claps sharply. "All right, girls. We will repeat the variation we learned last week, from the top." *Oh man. Not that one again.* "Indigo will demonstrate."

I take my place in the center of the room. The music starts and I'm already moving, my mind several seconds ahead of the music. I have to anticipate what comes next so I stay in time with the melody. Arabesque and hoooold. It feels like an eternity. I come out of the arabesque too early again. My tired body won't cooperate; my limbs feel like they're stuck in honey.

"Pull *up*, Indigo! Hold the arabesque!"

I move back across the floor, hit the arabesque again.

"Pull in the midsection! Breathe in!!" Miss Roberta is rabid.

My back muscles are screaming, legs all rubbery, the obvious and fatal signs of fatigue.

The music ends abruptly. "Indigo, this has got to stop. What is with you today? This is just sloppy and unacceptable. It won't cut it – here or anywhere else."

I stand crouched with hands braced on bent knees, catching my breath as her words rain down on my bowed head. I can't meet Miss Roberta's eyes. I know she's right. I place my hands on my thighs and bend over to catch my breath before responding.

"Marlene. Please come forward and show it from the top."

Marlene walks past me with her nose in the air. She takes her place in the center of the floor and the others back away to give her space. When our eyes meet in the mirror, she raises an eyebrow at me and smirks.

She performs the variation flawlessly.

Class ends and I scurry to the dressing room with my head still down. I throw my clothes on and root through my bag in search of my socks.

There's a loud *thump* to my left as someone slams their dance bag on the chair next to me. I don't have to look at it to know it's metallic purple with a blingy heart charm.

"How does it feel?" Marlene leans in close to speak in a low tone.

"I don't know what you're talking about." I don't look at her.

"Simple. You take something from me, I take

something from you."

"Like I said, I don't know what you're talking about."

"Don't think I don't see what you're up to. Jesse is mine," she snarls.

I look up at her and feel my eyes go buggy. "Are you kidding? People are not property. What is wrong with you?"

She snorts. "Today proves everything's right with me. Maybe you should be asking yourself what's wrong with *you*." She leans in so our faces are inches apart. "Back off while you still can or I'll take it all."

I jam my feet into my boots. "As if," I toss back at her on my way out.

During the ride home, Mom is eerily quiet. I sneak a glance at her, trying to get a read on her mood. Her face is puffy, the lines around her eyes more pronounced. I shift my gaze back to the road ahead of us, counting the minutes until I can get out of the car and put more space between us.

"Dad stopped by for a visit today."

I look at her face to see if she's joking, but she isn't. My grandfather abandoned my mother when she was five and she's spent much of her adult life trying to reconnect with him.

"How did that happen?"

"You know, it was just the oddest thing." Her face lights up. "He showed up out of the blue."

"I can't believe it," I say. I really can't. He has never been to our house.

"I couldn't either. I heard all this noise out front and saw this helicopter landing on the lawn. You can imagine how surprised I was when your grandfather hopped out."

She chatters on but I don't hear the rest because my mind is too busy doing the math, working out the probability of several equally disturbing scenarios: A) Mom fell asleep and dreamed all of this, B) Mom saw this on TV last night while she was wasted and thinks it really happened, or C) Mom is certifiably insane because she has permanently damaged her brain with alcohol.

Whichever version it is, she's completely delusional. Or a liar. Or both.

I close my eyes against the stream of lies pouring out of her lips.

"He said he's going to come back again in a couple of weeks. Isn't that wonderful?" She's so gleeful I almost expect her to start clapping her hands like a kindergartner. I stare at her incredulously.

"Great, Mom. Just great."

We cross Myer's Bridge and then we are home. I cannot get out of the car soon enough. I run to my room and shower under the hottest water I can stand and realize I have a pounding headache.

After, my body is sagging with fatigue so I lay down. My head throbs with each beat of my pulse. Then my phone rings.

"Hey, how are you?" Jesse's voice purrs at me.

"Okay, I guess." Part of me yearns to tell him about my crazy mother, but where would I even start?

"Cool, cool. Just wanted to hear your voice."

"That's a good thing."

He chuckles and then I hear a rumble of male voices behind him. "Hey, I'll call you later. We're going to catch the sunset. It should be epic."

Right then I hate him. For his easy life, his pack of friends, and his dimples. Also he definitely sleeps better than I do at night. He's half the reason I'm exhausted today.

"Right," I say. "Later."

chapter eighteen

The sun made a sudden appearance at the beginning of lunch hour. This is a major event in the Northeast, where it's critical to soak up every moment of winter sunlight. Bodies are strewn across the grass, clustered on the bleachers, leaning up against the side of the school.

The sun hurts my eyes as I exit the building. I look for Becky's head in the crowds but only see a few couples making out in the bleachers, and Brandon Moore, class clown since forever, shooting spitballs at everyone who walks by. A bunch of jocks are throwing a football.

I spot Becky under the giant maple, hunched over a fat textbook. She doesn't look up as I approach; she's writing while she reads, balancing her notebook on her lap while scribbling notes.

I think about how I know her...but not really. I've been eating lunch with her for more than a year. I know she tilts her head when she's listening – her little way of letting you know she's with you – and the funny way she grasps her pen, with all her fingers pressed together way down near the tip where the ink comes out. We've never had a deep discussion.

She's woven feathers into the ends of her hair today, which gives her an exotic look. The fringed top she's wearing looks like a watercolor painting; the colors mirror the blue skies and green hills behind her.

Talk to her. The voice in my head is so quiet, I think about ignoring it. I can't, though; I need to talk to someone or I'll go crazy. Becky's a logical choice. Her father made the headlines in the local papers a few years ago when they fished him, dead drunk, out of the hot tub at the YMCA. But even though my heart tells me it's the right thing to do, my head is tangled up with questions. Can I trust her?

Wind ruffles the pages of her book. She looks up and sees me standing there. "Hey. Take a load off," she says, patting the grass beside her. "I am so over pre-cal. Remind me why we need to know this stuff, again?"

"Umm...because they say so?"

"That's not a convincing enough argument." She laughs, slamming the book shut with a satisfying *thump.* "I'm putting it away."

"Can I talk to you?" For a second I wish Monique were here. But Monique is off in La-La Land with Austin right now.

"Sure. What's up?" Becky leans back on her palms.

"I feel like I'm losing it…"

The words flow like soda exploding out of a bottle. Becky's eyes widen as I tell her everything. I can't stand to hold on to it anymore.

When I stop talking, she is silent. Sounds surround us: the bouncing of a basketball on the asphalt court, gossiping voices, a slamming door. I wonder if I've said too much. Maybe she thinks I'm crazy. Maybe I am crazy.

"Wow, Indigo. I never would have guessed this was going on," she finally says. "But I'm glad you told me." She gazes out toward the edge of the woods. "Look, I know what you're going through – I've been there. I think you already know that. It isn't something I talk about."

"Especially here."

"Exactly." She looks at me. I don't see any judgment, just kindness and concern. "But talking about it helps."

Tears stream down my cheeks, but I can't stop them.

I feel her hand on my shoulder. "All it takes is one person to do something different, and the whole paradigm shifts. Like the butterfly effect." She gives my shoulder a gentle squeeze. "It'll be all right. You have to take the first step. Flap those wings and things will shift."

"Okay." It's just the barest whisper. I could use some wings.

The door squeaks loudly when I pull it open and heads turn. Of course we are late for this Al-Anon meeting. Coming here already feels weird; it's hard admitting that there's something wrong with my life. I can't imagine what anyone here could possibly say or do to help me. Aren't their lives just as messy and complicated as mine?

I see my reflection in the large picture windows. We are in some side room of a church I never attend. I really don't want to run into anyone I know. Metal chairs stand in a semi-circular formation around the podium. The overhead fluorescent lighting makes everyone look a little ill, and the musty air in this old building competes with the odors of coffee and sugary carbs. I notice several platters of donuts on a side table.

"Is anyone here for the first time?" says the green-suited woman at the podium. With her curly grey hair and wire-rimmed glasses she looks like someone's grandmother. I wonder which of her family members necessitated her being here.

Becky elbows me when I don't raise my hand. Reluctantly, I raise it.

"Your name, dear?"

I hate it when people call me "dear. " It reeks of condescension.

Becky looks at me accusingly.

"Indigo," I whisper.

The speaker clears her throat. "Welcome, Indigo." The others echo her welcome. "Bella will be sharing tonight."

Bella is a punky twenty-something wearing a lacy pale-grey dress and super dark lipstick. The frames of her glasses and her blunt-cut bob are the exact same shade of vivid fuchsia. Studded leather cuffs decorate her wrists and throat.

"Some of you know me, and others don't, so I'll start at the beginning." Her voice is faint and breathy, like Marilyn Monroe's. "I started coming to meetings because I felt helpless around my husband's drinking. There were dark days when I felt like my life was falling apart. I didn't want to talk to anyone else about it because I was too embarrassed. I felt completely alone. Eventually I realized that even if he wasn't going to change, I could change.

"It was hard to admit that I couldn't help my husband. I've learned that love sometimes means letting go and letting people make their own choices. We draw a line in the sand to keep clear boundaries – what we will and won't tolerate.

"I have to live my life, regardless of what he decides. I am responsible for my choices and he is responsible for his. I know where I am headed now, with or without him." Her teary eyes show the sadness behind the strength of her words.

I think about what she just said and my heart feels like a balled-up fist. What will I do if Mom refuses to get her life together? What would happen to me, Brad and Charlie? My mind races off in a million directions while other people in the room share their stories.

Their voices wash over me. Then I know why I am here. We all share something: we are a room full of people finding ways to cope while a loved one self-destructs.

The meeting closes with a prayer I've heard before, a prayer about serenity, changing what you can and letting the rest go. Chairs scrape the floor as people stand and cluster in little groups by the door.

I opt not to take any of the glossy pamphlets displayed neatly at the far end of the table: "Alcohol and Your Family" and "What to do When Someone You Love Drinks," with pictures of concerned-looking people on the front covers. Instead I grab some coffee. My hands need something to do. There isn't any milk, just evil non-dairy creamer, but there's no way I can drink it black.

It tastes bitter, like my thoughts, but I choke it down anyway while I swallow my anger. Something's become clear: I'm not taking Bella's route. I won't walk away from my family; I can't do that to my brothers. I'm not giving up. There has to be something else I can do.

I swallow the last drop of coffee and crumple my cup, then throw it in the trash. Becky links her elbow through mine as we head for the door. It's a comforting gesture; it pulls me back into my body and out of my spinning head. The door squeaks again as we leave.

Outside, the sky is an inky midnight blue. It's my favorite time, when the world hovers at the edge of night. A chorus of frogs chirps in the distance, echoing through the valley all around us.

"Did it help to come here tonight?" Becky's silhouette says in the almost-darkness.

"It helped to hear that other people are going through the same stuff. But I need a plan."

"Have you thought about an intervention?"

"What's that?"

"It's a meeting where family and friends confront the alcoholic and ask them to go to rehab… and give consequences if they don't agree."

"It sounds kind of like ganging up on the person. I'm not sure it would work."

"Well, it worked with my dad."

"What did you say to him?"

"I kept it really simple, you know? I said that I loved him and it was too hard watching him fall apart. If he didn't get help, I was going to go live with my aunt."

"What did he say?"

"At first he was shocked, but then he started crying. I think part of him was relieved because he didn't want to keep living that way. We drove him to rehab the next day."

"And then?"

"He was in rehab for a month. When he came home, he started going to AA meetings and got a sponsor and all that. He's been doing really well for almost two years now. It's like we got him back again. I don't think my parents would be together now if he hadn't gotten sober."

"I don't know if that would work with my mom."

"You never know unless you try, right?" She shivers. "C'mon. Let's get outta here."

Becky blasts the heat in the car. I hold my frozen fingertips in front of the heating vent, waiting for them to thaw. Light flickers through the cabin each time we pass a streetlight.

She parks in front of my house. "Are you okay?" I can't see her in the dark but I hear the concern in her voice.

"Yeah." I look at my house with a sinking feeling. I don't want to go in. I'd rather sit in Becky's warm car for the rest of my life, but I force myself to open the door. The overhead light shines on Becky and the edges of her hair glow like a halo.

"Call me anytime," she says. "I know it's a lot."

"Thanks. For everything." Darkness reclaims her

as I shut the door.

A second later she rolls down the window. "Oh yeah," she says. "I almost forgot. The most important part of an intervention is a unified group. It's not going to work unless your group is really together."

Great. Not only do I have to trek up the mountain, I've got to drag a whole heap of possibly unwilling people along with me. Including – no *especially* – my dad. How is that ever going to fly?

chapter nineteen

Christmas carols play softly in the background as we all watch Charlie tear into another gift. He tosses shredded silver paper in the large pile of wrapping paper cast-offs. His enthusiasm is contagious; I remember a flash of what it felt like back when I believed that Santa showed up in the middle of the night to deliver gifts. Charlie's a little too excited. He got all of us – even Dad – out of bed at 6:00 am.

"It's just a stinky t-shirt," Charlie says, tossing the shirt aside. The cartoon dinosaur on the front displays a wide set of enormous, pointy teeth.

Mom flashes Dad an irritated look, which he misses entirely. Dad wears his usual Christmas outfit: a red V-neck cashmere sweater and grass-green, wide-striped corduroys. A Santa hat sits at a jaunty angle on his head. Mom is in lavender velour sweats.

Charlie rips through three more gifts without pausing. He tosses them into his growing collection and goes over to the tree to search for more gifts.

"Charlie, how about we let someone else take a turn?" Dad suggests.

Charlie's shoulders droop like a day-old helium balloon. "Okay." He sits on the floor in a dejected heap.

Dad turns to Mom. "How about you, Hon? You haven't opened anything yet."

Brad hands her a package. We all watch her peel off the strips of tape and carefully unfold the paper. Mom is all about reusing paper. This sounds like an environmentally conscious thing to do but it's completely annoying when you have to sit through it with every present.

"Socks," she says. Her voice is devoid of emotion, her face pale and crumply without makeup. "Thanks, Hon," she says, giving Dad a perfunctory kiss.

Dad opens a stack of new underwear. "I really needed these. Thanks, guys."

Thirty minutes later there are only a few gifts left under the tree from long-distance relatives. I open a heart-shaped Cloisonné locket from my godfather. Brad scores a remote-controlled helicopter from his. The two boys disappear immediately to go try it out.

"Oh, Indy, I almost forgot your big gift from me," Mom says. "I have to go get it – it's upstairs."

She comes back to the room holding a black

garment bag in her hand. She's smiling for the first time all morning; she's put a lot of thought into this gift. For a split second I wonder if she bought me the outfit I'd circled in that cool catalog that came in the mail last month.

"Open it, open it," she says, putting the bag in my hands. "I can't wait for you to try it on."

I look at her for clues, but there's nothing. She's gone poker-faced. As I slide the zipper down, a quivery little feeling in my chest reminds me of that time when I got the dollhouse I'd been asking for.

My hands eagerly pull the bag open. I yank the hanger out of the top of the bag. My hand slides across...fur. Maybe it's that black coat I asked for with the detachable fur collar. I shove the garment bag off and pull the whole thing free.

Thing is the right word to use. It is a coat. At least I think it's a coat. It looks like a bunch of malnourished calico cats were slaughtered and stitched together. The fur sticks up at weird angles like the cats had a terrible fright just before they were killed. My heart sinks. It is the most horrible thing I have ever seen.

"Well, try it on," Mom says.

I struggle to hide my repulsion. I don't want to try it on. I will never wear it. I wouldn't be caught dead in it. But I can't tell her that. I am speechless. Some weird paralysis has taken over and I can't make the words come.

I paste a smile on my face. "It looks like it's the right size."

Her face falls. "You don't like it."

"No! I just didn't expect something like this, Mom. It's such a big gift."

It's too late. She knows.

"Well, let's get this place cleaned up," she says, a little too brightly. She grabs a pile of gift wrap and walks woodenly to the kitchen.

I watch her retreating back and I want the floor to swallow me up. But that doesn't happen. Instead I sit there, guilt crushing my shoulders, all the warm gushiness I felt swirling away like dirty bathtub water down the drain.

No one talks at dinner. The candles on the dinner table don't reveal the dark mood that has settled on all of us. The Christmas music sounds canned and fake. Hearing it now feels like some sort of sick joke.

Dad carves the roast beef. Mom always calls it Roast Beast, an inside joke she shares with Brad. My mind flashes on this thought and I have to stifle the completely inappropriate nervous laughter that tries to bubble to the surface. I still can't look my mom in the face.

I half-heartedly nibble on the steak and push the peas and stuffing around on my plate. I sneak a glance at Mom but she is pointedly ignoring me. She tosses back her last few sips of wine, then holds out her glass to Dad. "Can I get another splash, Hon?"

Brad and I share a look. The metallic twang of Charlie's fork scraping across his plate is bugging the crap out of me. His chewing sounds like farm animals have joined us at the table. I shove my hands under my thighs and look down at my plate to keep myself from saying something mean.

Mom serves a chocolate Christmas log for dessert. She calls it by its French term, *Bouche de Noël*, which always sounds pompous to me. The cake is decorated with a tiny forest scene; perky little deer and rabbits frolic in a glade of edible glitter. But even chocolate can't save this day.

Charlie scampers off to play with his new toys while Mom and Dad linger at the table drinking wine. Brad and I rinse the plates and stack them in the dishwasher. The second we are done, we fall into line like synchronized dancers, and silently exit the kitchen.

I fall on my bed and stare at the ceiling. As usual there are no answers there. My phone buzzes. A new message from Jesse. Written cryptically, as usual. I've never met anyone who was able to communicate with fewer words. All it says is: HOWZIT?

Where to begin?

I: BEEN BETTER

J: BEAT

I: EXACTLY

J: CALL U IN AN HOUR?

I: PRETTY PLS :)

My eyes have that burning, heavy feeling, so I close them.

A crash downstairs wakes me out of my alpha-state. Another crash has me hurrying down the stairs. When I'm halfway across the utility room I hear it.

"Fucking ungrateful kids! I am sick to death of every one of them!" Mom's voice is ragged with rage.

Dad's muffled reply is incomprehensible.

"Not one of them even said thank you! Bloody creeps! That's what they are!"

I hear Dad walk into the kitchen. The mechanical buzz of the ice-maker. Ice plinking into a glass.

Mom starts up again. "Don't you tell me to calm down! I'm not feeling calm!"

Another muffled response from Dad.

"Goddamn it, Jake! You're just as bad! And you're never fucking here!" Her voice is crazed.

An explosion – the sound of breaking glass scattering. A door slams.

Dad comes into the utility room and stops short, shocked to see me standing there. "Indigo, I—" He looks at his hands helplessly, like he's not quite sure they belong to him. "Uh, your mother had an accident...she, uh, dropped her glass. I need to clean it up before your brothers or the dog walk on it. Can you give me a hand?"

Mom's chair is on its side halfway under the dining room table. The tree leans against the wall like it's had one too many. Shards of broken glass cover the hearth, colored reflections from the Christmas lights winking off their surfaces.

"Jesus, Dad. What happened?" I realize I'm whispering, like I'm afraid to get caught.

"You know your mother," he replies.

"But Dad, this—"

"Look, Indigo, your mother is just tired. It's been a long week and it's late. Let's just get this cleaned up, okay?"

Every piece makes a loud *click* as it gets sucked into the vacuum. I feel shaky and nervous listening to it. The noise is so loud I expect her to come back screaming any second.

When it's done, I fall back into bed. My chest feels heavy, like there's an iron band wrapped around my diaphragm. Thoughts come in flashes, like a strobe light on overdrive. All of this is wrong. And underlining every one of these thoughts is a fear so huge I feel like I could drown in it.

My phone rings and I know it's Jesse, but I can't bring myself to answer it. If he heard my voice right now it would give everything away. I don't want him to know. I don't want anyone to know. I just want it all to go away.

Here's the message I would write if I could make myself write the whole truth and nothing but the truth: THIS FAMILY IS BROKEN.

chapter twenty

The moment Mom's car disappears from the driveway the air in our house takes on a different quality, like we can breathe again. Even Dad is more relaxed.

"Hey guys," he says, grinning widely. "I am on lunch duty today. Who's up for Chinese?" He gets a unanimous roar of approval, since Chinese is a rare treat for us.

When there are only a few scraps left, we read our fortunes aloud. Dad gets one about keeping friends close and enemies closer. Brad's suggests staying open to new opportunities. We put Charlie's torn halves together to read: "Good to begin well, better to end well."

"What about yours, Indigo?" Dad asks.

"A delightful surprise is in store for you soon," I say, striking a pose.

The phone rings while we're cleaning up. Since Mom's not around we are free to answer our phones without getting yelled at. This also means answering the phone is a contest. Brad and I both dive for it, but he's quicker.

"Stevens residence," he drawls, leering at me suggestively. "May I tell her who's calling?" His eyebrows rise. "Hold just a moment, please," he says, hamming it up with a completely fake and ridiculous British accent. He holds the phone out to me, then jerks it away at the last second when I reach for it.

"*Give* me that, you cretin." I wrestle the phone from him and walk away. I keep walking until I can't hear him snickering anymore.

"How good would you say you are with balance?" Jesse's voice makes me smile immediately.

"Um, excellent? If not I'd better switch careers."

"Care to put that to the test?"

"Why? What are you up to?"

"I'll tell you when I see you."

Overhead speakers blare cheesy pop music, the kind that easily embeds itself in your brain against your will. You know the melody and the words but would never admit it. Still, you catch yourself humming along or, even worse, bobbing your head to the beat. The current tune, "Drive Me Down," is one of my all-time love-to-hate favorites. Now it will be stuck in my head for days.

Jesse hands me my rental skates and bends down to slip on his own.

"Skates are a whole lot harder to put on than pointe shoes," I say, struggling with the laces.

"Let me help you." He bends over, revealing the back of his neck, which looks…edible. He tugs on the laces and his delicious, spicy scent rises my way. "You just need to start near your toes and tighten from there."

"Easy for you to say. You've had years of practice."

Saturday nights at the ice skating rink are cheerful, even though it's lit with fluorescents. Never flattering lighting, especially for a first date. The other skaters don't notice as they race by with huge smiles plastered on their grey, washed-out faces.

I didn't have the heart to tell Jesse that I suck at skating. Or that I have been expressly forbidden to try it. Then again, I'm pretty sure boys are on that list, too.

But when he told me what he had planned for our first date he was so excited. I couldn't possibly say no. The rules can take a hike for one night. Anyway, I'm no dummy; I know I'll have to hold on to him *a lot* just to stay upright. I just hope I don't end up looking like a total spaz.

He stands and offers me his hand, which I clasp gratefully. I'm already wobbling like a newborn giraffe and I'm not on the ice yet. I approach the ice slowly, moving extra cautiously, hopefully without looking demented. I almost hear Miss Roberta now. *I told you, Indigo, there are rules for serious dancers, and now you know why.* Then I freak out. What if I fall and damage something important?

"Shut up, Miss Roberta," I mumble.

"What was that?" Jesse asks.

"Nothing." I clasp his forearm with both hands as my first blade touches the ice and...*squeeeal* as my feet threaten to slip out from under me. Squealing is my father's least favorite noise on the planet (don't ask me why) but Jesse doesn't even flinch. For a second I am all windmilling arms and spastic footwork. Jesse steadies me with his other arm and I giggle uncontrollably.

He smiles. "Been awhile since you've been on the ice?"

"Yeah, you could say that," I reply.

The music takes a turn. If this were a school dance it would be a slow dance. The overhead lights abruptly shift to mood lighting. Colorful splashes of purple and fuchsia shimmer across the walls. A disco ball I hadn't noticed before throws out random streaks of light.

It sets the mood, turns it into a cinematic moment, like I am watching the whole thing on a big movie screen, a spectator to my own life. I feel weightless, like I'm fluttering through the rink on gossamer wings. I look over at Jesse, and he's staring at me intently. Cue the angel choir – I almost hear their echoing arias somewhere in the distance. His head dips nearer to mine. His eyes close.

The weightless feeling takes a new turn as my feet fly out from under me. For a second I really am weightless, as in *hurtling through space*. Time takes on that horrendous taffy quality, where every second stretches out into infinity. Even in the dark I can see Jesse's shocked face mirroring my own surprised horror as I barrel towards a clump of skaters directly in front of us.

I fall on my right hip, skidding across the ice, and take out the whole group like bowling pins.

When I look up, there's a circle of unfamiliar faces around us. Jesse's face looks anxious as he helps me sit up. "Are you all right?"

I nod slowly. I'm still disoriented, like the planet tilted and my brain got knocked around. But then I feel it. My ankle. It really, really hurts.

"My ankle. I think I twisted it or something."

He looks worried. "We'd better get you off the ice. Do you think you can walk on it?"

"I don't know."

He offers me his hand and hauls me to my feet. I wince with pain the second I put weight on my foot. I close my eyes.

"Hold on to me," he says, wrapping my arm around his neck. In one fluid motion he scoops me up and carries me off the ice. He makes his way to a bench, setting me down and settling himself beside me. "We need to get your skates off," he says. "Before it swells."

There's a searing pain as he frees my foot from the skate. The ankle looks swollen. I stare at it like it's not mine.

"Can you move it?" he asks.

I try, gingerly. It hurts but it still moves. It isn't broken. My eyes feel hot and burn as tears threaten to spill.

Someone brings an ice pack.

"Indigo, you need to ice it right away." Jesse's voice sounds far away, like he's talking through a tube.

So stupid. I never should have done this.

He sighs and gently pulls my foot in his lap. A minute later I feel the cold burn of the ice. "Man. I can't believe you're hurt. I'm so sorry," he says.

Me too. Plus now I hate myself.

"Coach always tells us to remember the rice method."

"Rice?"

"Yeah. It stands for rest, ice, compression and elevation. It's what we do for injuries."

Injuries. Miss Roberta was right. And now I'm going to have to explain to her what happened. And face the terrible music. And—

Jesse's hand briefly caresses the back of my

neck. He wraps an arm around my back and pulls me tightly to him.

He peels off his coat, revealing a moss-green sweater that matches his eyes perfectly. It looks soft enough that all I want to do is put my head on his chest.

So I do.

chapter twenty-one

When I open my eyes the next morning I almost forget what happened. Until I move my ankle. The twisted-up sheets and blankets pulling on it doesn't help. I grimace and roll over to one side, ripping the sheets away from my body. Time to survey the damage in broad daylight.

The swelling has gone down some, but it's still tender when I touch it. I try standing. That works. Mostly. But the reality of how much I've messed up sends me straight back to bed. I stuff pillows under it to prop it up. I grab my biology book from the bedside table. Maybe I can pack in an hour or two of studying since I'm stuck here anyway. The ceramic owl lamp next to my bed scowls disapprovingly.

"What are you looking at?" I mutter.

Great. I am definitely losing it. I'm talking to lamps.

My phone trills a new text message alert.

M: DID YOU HEAR?

I: NEGATIVE. WHAT R U TALKING ABOUT?

M: PAR-TAY

I: ?

M: SARAH BDAY :)

I: WHEN? WHERE?

M: SATURDAY, HER HOUSE

I: CALL U LATER TO DISCUSS?

M: K

I sigh and turn my focus back to coelenterates, but the words all blur together. The phone rings.

"Indigo." Miss Roberta's voice is crisp on the other end when I answer. "We need to have a little tête-à-tête. Do you want to go to the movies?"

A personal invitation from Miss Roberta? This is unprecedented. I've never spent time with her outside of ballet class before. But any invitation that gets me out of the house is welcome – even a football game or a monster truck rally.

"I'd love to, Miss Roberta, but my parents have this rule about us staying home on Sundays."

She exhales. "Put your mother on the line for a moment."

Miss Roberta must be awfully skilled on the phone because half an hour later I am climbing into her tiny, red, Japanese car. The car is just like her: pert and zippy. I hold my breath and remind myself not to limp to the car. I ease into the front seat; it was designed for people under five feet tall. Like clowns and six-year-olds.

She frowns slightly as she watches me get in. I brace myself, waiting for her to call me out. I wrapped my ankle tightly and wore my tall boots to cover the bandage.

"Remind me to make sure your parents never enter the halls of the New York School of Ballet," she says. She smoothes her eyebrows into shape in the rearview mirror before continuing. "We don't want to give them the impression you come from a family of basketball players. They'll pass you over, thinking you'll be too tall to be a ballerina."

"What?!" I screech, and she winces. I've forgotten the rule about using my inside voice in small spaces. "We're going to New York?"

"Of course. Didn't your mother tell you?"

"No. She didn't say anything about it."

Miss Roberta frowns. "Well. I hope she'll remember that your audition is in two weeks." She turns to me and her gaze softens. "But you did it, Indigo. You are ready. This is a celebratory outing."

My brain and body start to hum as she continues talking.

A new message pings. From Jesse.

J: BETTER TODAY?

I turn off the ringer and bury my phone deep in my purse. I silently swear to obey Miss Roberta's rules from now on. I am going to New York and nothing can stop me.

Miss Roberta expertly navigates the freeway. I watch the stark outlines of leafless trees zip by faster and faster. Everything – the clouds, the sky and the road – is the same monotonous grey. Even with the most depressing winter scene just outside the window, hurtling through space with Miss Roberta makes it all fade away.

Armed with a (small) bucket of (unbuttered) popcorn and a bottle of water each, we pick our way past the scattered limbs of gangly teens, little kids with runny noses, and one screaming infant. Definitely not the crowd I'm used to when I go to the movies, but then again, it's been awhile since I've seen a family movie.

The red velvet seats are scratchy. But I'm free, an unexpected luxury on a Sunday. I slouch back in the seat and close my eyes for a moment. My shoulder blades ache, right where my wings would be, if I had them, like I've been flying all night, an angel in overdrive. The weight of everything presses on my shoulders: New York, my mother, my GPA...and all the other details life keeps throwing at me.

The lights dim and my eyelids sag like they weigh a million pounds. A kaleidoscope of colored lights flickers across my lids, and I shake myself awake as the movie starts. *Mary Poppins* is not a movie I'd intentionally choose, but we could use her at our house; she could snap her fingers and fix all of our problems.

The characters are happy as they romp and dance across the screen. I wouldn't mind living in their colorful imaginary world. Maybe I could find that lucky chimney sweep and shake his hand...

The next thing I know, the credits are rolling. I must have fallen asleep without realizing it.

Miss Roberta looks at me, her brows a V of concern. "Are you getting enough sleep, Indigo? You seem tired lately."

"I'm fine." I answer feebly.

"Really." She looks at me searchingly. "Is there anything you want to talk about?"

I'm not sure what to say. On the one hand I feel like I could use some help from a rational adult, but on the other hand, if I tell her anything, my mom will have my head and make good on her threat to take away ballet. I press my lips together to keep them from spilling anything that could get me in trouble.

I answer vaguely. "I've just got a lot on my mind, you know. School, auditions, performances..."

"And home?" Her eyes shoot little daggers. Miss Roberta is no dummy.

"It's not always perfect." I sigh.

"I know. I see how you carry yourself in class some days. When your shoulders slump a certain way, I know things are difficult for you." She puts a hand on my shoulder. "I'm happy you are auditioning for New York, Indigo. You have a lot of talent, and you could go far. But every talent needs the proper environment to grow and flourish. I want you to know that I've had a little talk with your mother. I told her not to drop you off at ballet class crying again. You need to stay focused on where you are headed without unnecessary distractions."

All the air is gone from my lungs. What has Miss Roberta done? My headache intensifies, like someone's cranked up the volume. I gulp audibly.

But now I know there's one more pair of eyes watching over me. And my mother.

Brad idly bounces a basketball in the driveway when Miss Roberta drops me off. As she pulls away I notice there's a huge pile of random stuff on the lawn: broken toys, clothing, the odd book or two. Then I see Fluffy Bear, Charlie's favorite stuffed animal, half-buried under a shoe. Cold, hard dread lodges in my ribcage.

Brad launches into dialogue, confirming my suspicions. "You are so lucky you weren't here this afternoon," he says, looking grave. He stops bouncing the ball and stares at the ground, his expression clouding over.

"What happened?" I ask with a sinking feeling.

"She totally freaked out. Over nothing. She went upstairs and Charlie hadn't made his bed yet...and—"

"And what?" My heart is beating erratically.

"Then she totally went after him and started throwing all his stuff out the window. Now she's acting like he deserves it." His shoulders sag. "This sucks. She sucks. I don't know what to do."

Frustration makes me want to hit something. I make a fist and bite on one of the knuckles so I don't scream. It doesn't seem to matter how hard we try to keep the peace, the punishments just keep on coming, and they're getting worse. Poor Charlie.

"Where is he?"

"Upstairs in his room. She told him to stay there until she said he could come down."

I start walking.

"I wouldn't go in there right now if I were you," Brad warns.

I brace myself and go inside anyway. The house is completely quiet, like it's waiting to see what my next move will be.

Charlie's door is closed, so I knock on it softly. "Hey, bud, you in there?" I open the door after his muffled response.

He's lying on his side on the bed, facing the window with his back to me.

"Can I sit next to you?" He doesn't respond, so I walk to the other side of the bed and sit next to him gently. His face is puffy and drawn; his knees are pulled into his chest, either for comfort or protection. He looks at me and I pet his head slowly. "You would have liked the movie," I tell him. "We'll have to rent it sometime. It has all these great songs and the characters jump into a painting and visit a magical land. Doesn't that sound cool?"

Charlie closes his eyes and nods wanly.

"Are you all right? Brad told me what happened."

He rolls onto his back and shuts his eyes. Then I see it. A large, purple, mottled bruise blooms across his right arm. It is hand-shaped. Each of her fingers made an indelible petal of pain.

I continue to rub his head and talk. "Don't worry, I'm going to fix this. In the meantime, you stick with Brad and me, okay? No running off by yourself."

His rhythmic breathing and the steady rise and fall of his chest tell me I am talking to dead air.

I find Dad in his office, hunched over a pile of papers. "You're back," he says, looking up at last. "How was the movie?"

"Great." Enough small talk. My anger flares. "Dad,

what happened with Charlie?"

"The usual. He's always getting into some fool thing that doesn't concern him. This time he went too far and your mother let him have it."

"Let him have it? Dad! She tore apart his room and destroyed everything. And that makes sense to you? That's okay?"

"Look, your mother did what she needed to do. You know she's ready to put him on medication as it is. He needs to control himself."

"She's crossed a line, Dad."

"Look, I'm not asking you to like it.

"But Dad—"

"It's over. I'm through talking about it."

I retreat to my room, feeling dizzy with confusion. I sit on the bed and wait for my head to clear. Then I see it in the corner: my own pile of ruined belongings. My collection of CDs, shattered and broken, my new leotard with the lacey back panel in shreds. I don't know what to do with the anger that's threatening to buzz out of my skin. I feel like screaming.

Words bubble to the surface. Something has to change. But what can I do? I have to talk to someone or I'll go nuts.

Monique picks up, sounding breathless. "Hey, Sugarplum. What's the 4-1-1?"

"I was going to ask you the same. What are you up to?"

"Austin and I—" She giggles insanely. "Stop it,

you!" Muffled sounds of struggle. "Okay, sorry. Where was I?" More giggling. "Austin has graciously offered to take me on a surprise date somewhere. I know not where. I will go…*If*—" she laughs, "—and *only if* he behaves while I'm talking to you."

"Surprise date? Sounds very romantic." I try to sound upbeat while my heart plummets.

"Totally. I love his romantic streak. I think I might keep him." An unintelligible reply from Austin. "Yes, I said *might*." Another muffled reply. "You're right. I am crazy about you. Although I'm not always crazy about your *behavior*." Kissing sounds. "Indy, I gotta fly. I'll see you tomorrow, K? Be good, that way at least one of us will be! Love you." And just like that, she is gone.

I look at the clock. Only fourteen more hours until I might get another chance to talk to her.

I need a Plan B.

chapter twenty-two

Monique holds center stage at lunch the next day. Even Sarah listens intently for a change, nodding enthusiastically as Monique gives us the play-by-play of her weekend with Austin. I will myself to listen and not obsess about the bruise on Charlie's arm or New York, or on my ankle.

It felt better when I woke up this morning but it still isn't right. With the audition less than two weeks away there's not much time. Maybe I'll be okay soon if I ice it every morning and evening. Plus I'm doing contrast baths, alternate ice and hot water to force blood to flow into the area so it heals more quickly.

"...don't you think, Indy? Isn't love amazing?" Monique looks at me expectantly.

More like dangerous, if you ask me. "You seem really happy. You deserve it," I reply. I am glad for her and I'm sure love is great, for people who can afford the risk.

Monique leans forward. "Sunday he took me to this really great spot..." I can't listen anymore but there isn't a nice way to exit without her noticing so I play last week's variation over in my head.

There's a squeal of chairs and I look up to find my friends staring at me quizzically.

Becky looks confused. "Aren't you coming, Indy?" She starts walking and I follow her down the hall, struggling to stay by her side. Art class is the only time when Becky isn't late. I spot Jesse in the crowd of people up ahead. He waves and I pretend not to notice. I turn to Becky. "Go ahead, I'll meet you. I've got to duck in here a second."

Duck? More like chicken. I scurry into the girls' bathroom and lock myself in a stall. My heart is pounding as guilt washes over me. I remind myself that New York is just around the corner. *Single point of focus, Indigo. No distractions.*

I stay there until the bell rings.

Miss Roberta zeros in on my ankle the second I walk into the studio. "What," she says, "is that?" Her eyes bulge as she takes in the bandage.

"It's nothing, Miss Roberta. I just—"

"You're injured. That's not nothing. How did this happen?"

"It was stupid. I was running around with my brothers and I twisted it." The lie comes out so smoothly it surprises me.

She sighs. "You know you have to be careful. Especially now."

The concern in her voice makes me feel ten times worse. I slither over to my spot at the barre. Monique gives me a questioning look but I keep my gaze elsewhere.

All through barre I mentally kick myself for bending the rules every time I feel a twinge in my ankle. I flat-out hate myself when I have to sit and watch jumps.

When class is finally over I dress in silence, ignoring the stares from the other girls. I shrug into my coat and head for the stairs without looking back.

"Indy! Wait up!" Monique's voice follows me down the stairs. "Hey, girl. Slow down. I want to talk to you." I hear her boots clomping after me.

"Not here. Outside," I say without stopping.

Once we hit the cold night air, I pull her around the side of the building. No need to have the entire class know what an idiot I am.

Monique pulls away from me. "You're acting really weird. What's going on?"

"I did something kind of stupid and I'd rather not have it become public knowledge, okay?"

I tell her about my date with Jesse and how I injured myself. "But there's more… Miss Roberta took me to the movies yesterday, which was the day after I went skating with Jesse—"

"Wait. You had a date with Miss Roberta?" she says. "That doesn't make any sense."

"At first I thought it was strange, too, but it was a celebration. She's taking me to New York in two weeks! I'm finally going to audition!"

"Two weeks! Indy, that's unbelievable! Wait. that's like no time at all…" She covers her mouth, trying to hide her expression of horror. "Crap! What are you going to do?"

"Nothing. I'm going to do absolutely nothing that isn't related to ballet and the audition."

"But what about Jesse? Does he know?"

"No, he doesn't."

"Aren't you going to tell him?"

Do I need another mother? That would be a no. I sigh. "We went on one date. He doesn't own me. I'll figure something out."

When Jesse calls later that night, I ignore it and force myself to do one hundred extra stomach crunches.

When I hear the beep that indicates a new voicemail, I do two extra sets of leg lifts and enough bridges to make the backs of my thighs burn.

And when I get in bed and close my eyes and see his face, I do nothing.

chapter twenty-three

Two weeks pass by in a flurry of extra practice sessions with Miss Roberta, extra exercises every night, and a mountain of ignored texts and voicemails from Jesse. I feel a twinge of guilt when I think about how confused he must be, but then I turn my attention back to packing my things for tomorrow's audition.

I lay out my favorite leotard, a lavender-grey camisole with multiple crisscross straps. It will go perfectly with the rhinestone comb from Becky. As I work my way down Miss Roberta's checklist, I cross off each item as I put it in the bag. Miss Roberta gives new meaning to the word thorough. I've got snacks, a sewing kit, extra shoes, extra tights, extra everything. I've even got pharmaceuticals (Band-Aids, antibiotic ointment, aspirin). I could go live in New York for the next week with all the stuff I've got in here.

It's after 10:00 pm when I finally collapse into bed. I hug myself in anticipation; ten hours from now I'll be on the train with Miss Roberta.

It takes eons to fall asleep.

I have the dream again. It's the same one I've had since the summer I was ten and there was a shark sighting at the beach. Sharks swirl just below the water's surface, giant grey torpedoes with mouths like saws. The dream always leaves me with the same cold feeling of terror I felt that summer when the ocean became a dark, unreadable thing and I was too afraid to dip a toe in the water.

Danger.

It's here. I don't feel any better with my eyes open, heart pounding in the darkness, the sheets a tangled fury at my feet.

In the meantime I can kiss sleep goodbye. More lost hours of rest. Just the thought stresses me out. I close my eyes and say a fervent prayer. *Help me.* Even though I'm not sure I really believe in that stuff, it can't hurt to try.

But then I see it. Light coming from my parents' room at the end of the hall. I blink, my mind still groggy with sleep. A quick glance at my bedside clock tells me it is the middle of the night.

Something doesn't feel right. I hastily toss the covers aside. I slide my feet into my furry slippers and head down the hall towards my parents' room, past the ceramic lawn jockey that used to terrify me when I was a kid.

When I get to my parents' room there's no sign of them anywhere. Every light in the room is on. I shiver as another childhood nightmare resurfaces: my parents disappeared from the house at night and I found them outside, crouching high in the treetops like animals, their eyes glittering strangely. This feels eerily similar.

I'm hearing things, too. Voices seem to be coming from the wall near the window that overlooks the giant oak tree in front of the house. I move closer, half expecting to see my parents out there in the tree.

The window is open slightly – an old summer camp habit of Dad's that refuses to die, no matter the season. The man has to have fresh air when he sleeps.

I hear Dad's voice down below. The floodlights are all on outside, beaming down the whole front walkway. Dad stands under one of the beams like he's on stage. He's wearing his bathrobe and slippers, deep in conversation…with a policeman.

Were we robbed? Is someone hurt? My mind attempts to come up with some sort of reasonable explanation for why a policeman is in our front yard in the middle of the night. Then I hear it: a strange noise, half groan, half creak. A sound that belongs in a horror movie…not on my front lawn.

My eyes trace the giant skid marks gouged across our lawn to the source of the noise: my mother's car, balanced precariously at the water's edge like a child's teeter-totter. But this is no toy; it's a grown woman's all-wheel drive Audi station wagon, centimeters away from ending up in the lagoon.

A tow truck pulls up the driveway, and in the beam of its headlights, I see my mother with another policeman, walking the length of our driveway as she struggles to walk a straight line to prove her sobriety. The policeman shakes his head. An animated conversation ensues, Mom full of overdone laughter and dramatic gestures.

This ought to be good. Maybe now Dad will finally get a clue.

chapter twenty-four

"You know I don't see well at night," Mom announces the next morning. She sets a bowl of oatmeal in front of Charlie. He grimaces. Charlie hates oatmeal.

She waves her hands like she's sweeping it all away, like it's nothing. Dad nods distractedly behind his newspaper. *Hello, Dad, denial much*? I telegraph my anger but it goes straight over his head. His newspaper has some sort of invisible force field.

Mom nods like it's all settled and heads off to the kitchen. I glare at her retreating back. She turns suddenly as her mom radar kicks in. She catches my look and glares at me. She's even smug. Or maybe that's just my "attitude" talking.

I sit silently, squelching the nasty words that threaten to fly out. My chest knots up in a tight ball and an unending stream of questions bubble up in my mind: so that's it? She's just going to get away with it? What did she say to the cops?

Most importantly, how can Dad fall for such a lame excuse?

Moments later I smell the faint scent of a cigarette. She always smokes when she's in planning mode with the family calendar. That scent is her signal to stay away; she hates being interrupted.

"Brad," she calls, "when is your next game?"

"Coach said it's Saturday."

"Crap," she says. "Now I'm going to have to move Charlie's speech therapy. Why can't they give us more notice for these games, dammit? And why the hell do they have to be at 6:00 am on Saturday? Like I don't have enough to do already. Now I have to haul my ass – and yours – out of bed at 4:30 am just to get you there on time!" She takes another drag of her cigarette and mutters under her breath.

I push my chair back abruptly and flee. I don't have time for this.

Upstairs in my room I angrily throw things in my dance bag. My mind keeps time with my motions. Hate. Her. Hate. Her.

"Do you want to tell me what the frack is going on?" Brad says from the doorway.

"Not now. Miss Roberta will be here any minute." I cram in my warm-up clothes and manage to jab myself on my sewing needle. "Oww! God *dammit!*" Brad shrinks away in surprise at my howl of frustration.

Mellow out, Indigo. He is not the enemy. The red veil tinting my vision evaporates.

"Later, okay?" I say. "We'll talk about everything later."

Charlie comes in and sits on my bed. He hugs my heart shaped pillow like he's hoping it will hug him back.

"This is getting old," Brad says. "We need a plan."

"Maybe we could get a new mom," Charlie suggests.

I sigh. "I know it sucks. I hate it. I hate her."

Their eyes go wide with fear. Tension crackles in the air like static electricity. And that's how I know she is there. Right behind me. And she heard everything I just said.

I turn slowly. She's standing in the doorway to my room, hands on her hips, jaw set tight, eyes narrowed.

Fear courses through my veins, cold and steely. My primal brain takes over; I know I'm in for a fight. Swallowing is a challenge. My limbs feel funny, like I don't quite have them under control. They're quivery and loose, and I feel a little bit like I'm floating.

My mind searches wildly for the right thing to say. Something sensible. No. Screw sensible. Sensible is what has gotten me into this mess in the first place, and I can pretty much bet she is not about to be sensible.

"You all have some nerve. I break my back for you and you are so ungrateful. You assholes are a disgrace, each and every one of you." Her voice is icy.

Something in me snaps. Hot bile rises from the

back of my throat. The acid taste makes me want to spit it in her face. "Look at them," I say, pointing to my brothers. "They cower like beaten dogs every time you walk by. Is that what you want?"

My breath comes in heavy, ragged gasps. We stare each other down. My brothers inch over to the wall, watching us.

Is it my imagination or does she grow larger when she's pissed? "Do you think any of this is easy?" She screams. "I never stop working. I am always tired. And why? Do you know how many miles I put on that damn car yesterday?? 117. One-hundred-and-seventeen miles. Driving all of you around to your activities. I continually pick up after all of you. Every meal is my responsibility. Try it some time and see how well you do."

"We know. You continually remind us of everything you do. But it always comes with a price."

"I can't wait for you to have kids. Then you'll understand. But in the meantime, it's my way or the highway, sister. End of story."

The red haze returns. I feel dizzy – I can't see her or my brothers anymore. It's as if everything has been covered with a crimson filter.

"I can't believe this! This is so messed up! *You* are the problem, Mom! You and your drinking!" The words come out before I can stop myself, my throat raw with the force behind the words.

Bright light. A sudden explosion. The side of my face hurts, the skin on my right cheek burns. She slapped me. Full force.

"What did you say to me?"

I rub my face and glare. "You heard me."

She jabs a finger at me. "You are done. Do you hear me? Done – no audition. No more ballet. You have crossed the line. Is that clear?"

I hate her so much I wish she would spontaneously combust. "No. *You* are done. Your drinking is ruining everything. Everything!"

I grab my bag and run but my body refuses to cooperate. My limbs are wooden with anger, like a puppet whose knee joints have locked up. I can't get away fast enough. I run down the stairs, slamming the back door as hard as I can when I leave.

Have to get out of here. Can't let her stop me. Not now.

I walk down the driveway. Fast. But it doesn't feel fast enough. I keep expecting to hear her behind me any second. I start running. Not down the road toward town; she'll find me for sure. I veer off through the trees on the hill behind Mrs. LaRue's house. My breath comes in heavy gasps as I run, tree limbs raking my clothes and skin. I feel like a lunatic, some ill fated muse with zero wilderness skills. I have to find Miss Roberta before Mom does. There's no way I'm missing this audition.

Once I'm over the hill I hit the road again and my boots thud on the pavement as angry energy buzzes through my insides. I can't believe she slapped me. The rules of this game are now clear. Mom verbally vomits

The train plunges into darkness for our final descent into Grand Central Station. I look out into the darkness, but there's nothing to see. It's pitch black and creepy out there. My reflection in the window is gaunt and hollow-eyed with yearning. I almost don't recognize my own face.

"Your tour jetés still need a little work, but hopefully she'll give something else for big jumps." Miss Roberta isn't helping my confidence right now. I look away.

"Last stop! Man-*hattan*!" The conductor's voice booms through the speakers.

We step off the train and into the swarm of people on the platform. We follow the masses into a huge room with marble floors and high ceilings covered in constellations. Clocks and huge electric timetables clutter the walls above the row of ticket windows on the opposite side of the room. We've reached the heart of Grand Central Station.

"Come on, this way." Miss Roberta grabs my hand and drags me up a giant staircase to the exit. We stand in the taxi line amidst the cacophony of honking car horns, bus engines, yelling voices and shoes clicking by on the pavement. The heavy exhaust fumes make my eyes burn. When it's our turn, I slide across the black leather seat inside the cab to make room for Miss Roberta. I breathe a sigh of relief. I'm exhausted and I haven't even done anything yet.

The taxi ride is an obstacle course. We race through several intersections and then crawl through crowded side streets. We drive by block after block of buildings so tall I can't see the top floors. New York is alive with movement and everyone moves quickly. High heeled women and well dressed men in smart suits power walk past us. Even grandmas walking miniature dogs hustle by.

At last the taxi pulls up to the curb. "66th and Broadway," the driver grunts. Miss Roberta pays him. He's bug-eyed in the photo on his taxi license which is prominently posted on the dashboard. Not exactly a flattering shot.

We exit the cab and Miss Roberta glances across the street. She takes a deep breath, as if to reorient herself. Her nimble fingers adjust her floral headscarf. "All right," she says, either to me or herself. "We have plenty of time, but we need to use it wisely. You must be flawless in both your appearance and your performance and thoroughly warmed up before the audition begins."

NYSB's building doesn't look like much from the outside: it's grey, boxy, and institutional; easy to overlook. We turn the corner and eight-foot tall bronze letters outside the front doors declare we have arrived at the New York School of Ballet.

During the ride up in the elevator, Miss Roberta reads through her last minute checklist. We exit at the third floor where the black linoleum floor has sparkly flecks in it, which feels a bit *Wizard of Oz-ish*. We enter through glass double doors that proclaim "New York School of Ballet" in flowing gold cursive.

"It's a good thing your parents didn't bring you here today," Miss Roberta says, looking around furtively.

"Why is that?"

"If they got one look at how tall your mother is, they would never accept you. In fact, it would be better if she never came here at all."

She never will. Not if I have anything to say about it. I can't imagine my mother wanting to come here, anyway. She has a complete phobia of Manhattan.

A grey looking receptionist with thick black glasses and a heavy accent tells us where to find the locker room. She is obviously Russian, like many of the teachers and administration at the school.

The butterflies increase as I push open the heavy locker room door. It creaks loudly in protest. Rows and rows of lockers and benches stretch out on all sides. A mirrored wall stands to my right. There is a white paper towel lying on the floor in front of it, displaying a cockroach the size of my thumb.

Feeling disgusted, I quickly look away and look for a spot to get changed. I have my pick since the locker room is empty. The shaky feeling worsens as I pull on my leotard and tights. The door squeaks again and two other dancers walk past as I grab my brush and go to the mirror, brushing my hair into a ponytail. More dancers arrive. The ponytail gets coiled and twisted into the prerequisite ballet bun. I pin my hair tightly to make sure it stays put during the audition, then I douse it all with hairspray and throw everything into my bag. It is freezing in here, so I throw on my ballet sweater and leg warmers.

A last glance in the mirror (while consciously ignoring the roach) shows a professional dancer.

When I exit the dressing room, Miss Roberta has a different opinion. "The jewelry needs to come off, every last bit of it, except your earrings. And what about those flyaway hairs? Wet them down and spray them flat before you go in." She narrows her eyes at the other dancers assembling in the hallway.

I avoid looking at the others; I don't want to psych myself out. I find a spot on the floor and begin warming up with gentle stretches.

"Are you auditioning in the first group?" a timid voice asks. I turn to face a delicate, rail-thin blonde. She is so skinny I can see every bone in her face. I can't imagine how she has enough strength to get through class.

"Yes. How about you?"

She nods. "I came from Missouri to try out. That's my mom over there on the couch." She points to a plump, middle-aged redhead. "My name's Lila." She looks at me, then the floor.

She is visibly trembling, she's so nervous.

"I'm Indigo," I say with a smile. "Missouri is a long way away from here. Weren't there any auditions closer to where you live?"

"Cincinnati was closest, but we couldn't make it the day they had an audition there. This ended up working out well because my whole family came along.

My dad and brother are checking out the dinosaur bones at the Museum of Natural History."

Miss Roberta waves at me suddenly, a small piece of paper in her hand – my number for the audition. "I'd better get going. It was nice meeting you, Lila. See you inside and good luck."

"Thanks. You, too."

Moments after my number is pinned to my leotard, we are called into the audition and I wave a temporary goodbye to Miss Roberta.

The studio is a dream. It's the largest and most luxurious ballet studio I've ever been in, at least four times the size of Miss Roberta's. I almost feel like I'm in a movie. Three rows of ballet barres run along the perimeter of the room, multiple levels to accommodate multiple heights. The front wall is completely covered in floor-to-ceiling mirrors. The wide expanse of smooth grey vinyl floor beckons. A glossy black grand piano stands in the far corner. A pianist sits in front of it, waiting attentively.

I can't believe it – a real live pianist instead of recorded music.

I find a spot along the barre next to the mirrors. I tuck my dance bag along the wall under the barre, leaving my water bottle on the floor next to it. I take a glance in the mirror and smooth my hair down one last time. Behind me the room is completely filled with other dancers stretching and primping. No one talks.

"Close the door." A stern female voice with a Russian accent cuts through the silence. She's dressed head-to-toe in black, a form-fitting calf-length skirt and sweater. She wears a strand of pearls around her neck and pearl earrings to match, like she's ready to go to a cocktail party. The only thing that gives her away as a dancer is her choice of footwear: half ballet slipper, half character shoe, an open ballet slipper with a low heel. Her face is wrinkled but her hair is a glossy blue-black, quite mesmerizing. She is old, but it's impossible to say exactly how old. Her eyes, by contrast, are deep green, clear, and penetrating. It's the type of gaze that doesn't just see everything; it sees *through* everything.

Madame Anna Kirowski has arrived.

The studious-looking receptionist stands next to her. She's wearing four-inch heels but the top of her head only reaches Madame K's shoulders. They converse in hushed tones, pointing at several dancers and nodding before bowing their heads back together in quiet conversation.

"Girls, ve vill begin!" Madame K barks, clapping her hands together. She strides heavily toward the piano and grabs the barre to demonstrate. She shows a plié combination, counting out each step in the face of our silence. "Vun and two. Vun and two."

We work. Perspiration starts to collect on the side of my face and under my breasts and armpits. With each exercise, we stand at attention, watching and straining to understand her as she shows us what to do next. We repeat each step countless times – a million tendus, jetés, and fondues. Our legs move forward, side, back and side in unison, all down the line as the pianist pounds out the tempo.

Sweat pours down my face, chest, and legs. The barre will be over soon. When I turn my head to sneak a quick glance, my face is red in the mirror.

Grand battements at last. It's a relief to be finishing the barre but now it's time for the center of the floor. Soon they'll start cutting people one by one.

Madame K stops and says something to me but her words make no sense. I look at her blankly, unable to utter a sound. What does she want?

"Yourrr fute," she says. "Geev me yourrr fute." She looks exasperated. She tries another tactic. "Point toe here." She points in front of her feet.

I slide my right foot on the floor where she indicated and she grabs it and wrenches it above my head as far as it will go. She holds it there while she has another private, guttural Russian conversation with the receptionist. The hot metal burn in my hamstring tells me that this is my limit. At last, she releases it.

"Goot." She gives me a quick nod.

I'm shaken. I feel slightly violated. That was kind of weird, but being singled out is supposed to be a good thing. I think.

Then we are moving across the floor and I feel myself flowing, blooming. When I glance at myself in the mirror, I look…like I'm supposed to be here. But do I stand out enough from the rest of the dancers? I decide to set this question aside for now.

By the time we put on pointe shoes our group is now half the size it was when we started the audition.

We pirouette and the sweat flies, droplets flung to all sides each time I spin and find my eyes in the mirror. We start jumps. Fluttery footwork first, we are birds skimming across the floor, lighter than gossamer. When bigger, grander jumps follow, I push myself to hang suspended, to defy gravity a millisecond longer than everyone else.

Until there is nothing left but the biggest jumps of all.

She walks through a tour jeté combination and points to me. "You show," she says.

The blood rushes to my head. I hear it pounding in my ears as the music begins. Then I imagine Miss Roberta reminding me to jump like gravity has no hold on me. This is why she's been making me do the extra leg exercises at home. Now as I dance, it seems to have lost its grasp. I float through the air and jump with every last tendril of strength I have. I've never jumped so high. The heady cocktail of anger, burning desire, and adrenaline flows through me, turbo-charging every move. I don't look at anyone else. I definitely don't look in the mirror.

Right then, my shoe starts to slip. I am only a few measures away from finishing but it continues to slip. I didn't rosin my heels. So stupid. I can't stop. *Keep going, Indigo.* No matter what, I can't stop. It slides further and further off my left heel and I silently curse it. Tombé, pas de bourrée…it is almost completely off. The ribbons strain against my ankle, cutting into the flesh through my tights. I grit my teeth and keep going.

A final grand jeté, and I land. All wrong. On the loose shoe. It buckles underneath me and the floor below my feet goes wobbly. And then I am on my knees. In front of everyone.

The room is silent. Madame K doesn't say a word, but looks at me for a moment, her green eyes flashing.

I've ruined everything. Miss Roberta will be so disappointed. I can't tell her that I forgot to rosin my shoes in place. *So sloppy, Indigo.* My mind is full of too many things and I've lost my focus, my edge. Spacing out on this one little thing could cost me everything.

I pick myself up in silence and sit on the sidelines while I fix my shoe, retying the ribbons so tightly, they cut into my skin. The rest is a blur. I go through the final motions but collapse on the inside until we are released.

Outside in the hall, I refill my water bottle from the fountain and gulp down water as Miss Roberta peppers me with questions.

"Did she single you out in any way? Were you able to keep up? What did you think of the other girls?"

I answer by nodding and shaking my head. I can't bring myself to speak.

I won't tell her. I just won't. Whatever happens from here is mine to accept, for better or worse. My head is spinning and my legs feel rubbery, like they might suddenly give way. I might melt into a big puddle right here in the middle of the hall. I don't want to talk; I just want to sit down. Actually, I want to get back on the over-refrigerated train and go home to Connecticut. And sleep.

"We won't know anything for a few weeks," Miss Roberta says when we are safely back on the train. I am trying to get comfortable, but it's impossible in these seats. Who designed these freaking seats? Looking across the aisle at the opposite row of seats, I can see why: the design is all wrong. The seats are curved into a slight C-shape, exactly the opposite of proper posture. No one sits in that shape – slumped over, head jutting forward. Or at least they're not supposed to. But that is exactly the position that all of these seats force you into.

"In the meantime, we work," she continues. "Getting into the program is just the first step. After that, you'll need to work smarter and harder than the rest of the class. You will have to live in New York," she says matter-of-factly.

Live in New York? I stifle the urge to laugh. That's not going to happen for me. I've blown my one chance to finally be in charge of my own life.

The Big City was loud, dirty, and crowded, but it was like a breath of fresh air for me, far away from the stifling existence of living in Connecticut. New York is *the* place for serious dancers who are ready for a professional career, and I want that more than anything.

Can I imagine it? Yes. I can taste it, and I want it all: stern Russian leaders; live piano music for every class; huge, open and airy studios…even the locker room, with its unbelievably large and disgusting insect population. I want it because I want to dance…more than anything.

And now it's all slipping away from my fingers, mile after mile, as the train hurtles on towards home.

Home: horror. Of. My. Existence. That's what home stands for. And now I'm stuck with it for at least another year. Maybe forever.

My eyelids begin to feel heavy with the gentle swaying of the train. Nothing can keep me from drifting off – not the uncomfortable seats, the frozen temperature or my own excitement.

I sleep until Miss Roberta shakes me awake at our stop.

chapter twenty-five

When I awake, the sky is a pallid wash of grey, brightened slightly from its reflection off the few patches of remaining snow outside. In other words: depressing.

I get out of bed, but I already have a sinking feeling of dread. Miss Roberta told me to take the day off today and relax after the audition. Plus I'm grounded for the rest of my life for mouthing off to Mom. Now I'm stuck at home, such an anticlimactic way to finish an otherwise brilliant weekend. I can't stop replaying the audition in my head, contemplating how New York is clearly over for me before it even got started.

I grab a bowl of crisped rice. It's my last ditch

effort to pick up my mood. But today they are silent in the bowl – not a single snap, crackle, or pop. Figures they'd be stale. One more reason this day already sucks.

There's a knock at the window and I look up. Monique smiles broadly, then makes a series of ridiculous faces and gestures for me to meet her at the front door.

When I open the door, she bursts in, stamping her feet. "Man, it's arctic out there."

I put my finger to my lips, shushing her.

"What?" she says, too loudly. "What *is* it with you, Indy? How was the audition? You should be celebrating! Come on, girl. I'm taking you out for coffee – Austin's waiting in the car. He's got the heat blasting and everything."

I break the bad news to her.

"Beat," she says. "Your mom sucks."

I shush her again.

"All right, all right. Geez. You know I don't do 'quiet' well." A puzzled look crosses her face. "But Indy, what about Sarah's party tonight?"

"It's obvious, M. I can't go."

She motions me closer. Cups her hand around my ear and enlightens me.

Becky can't find parking anywhere near Sarah's

house so we end up parking a half mile down the road under a giant weeping willow tree. The leaves rustle a papery shiver in the wind as we start walking.

Becky shakes her head. "How many people did she invite? The whole school?"

The wind picks up again and I shiver. "Let's hurry. It's freezing out here." I link my elbow through hers and race/walk toward Sarah's, imagining my mom with the rabid face of a werewolf running at my heels. That's how much trouble I'll be in if she realizes I snuck out.

Music blares as we come in through the huge double doors of Sarah's house. The place is packed, bodies curled up on the couches, others standing in groups. There's a crowd dancing over by the window, their movements eerie in every frozen pop of the strobe light.

We stand here, uncertain about where to go, looking for a familiar face. I spy Monique and Austin curled up together, lip-locked on the loveseat over by the television.

Becky and I share a look. "C'mon," she says. "Let's go look for Sarah." Becky heads for the kitchen and I trail behind her.

There's a half-empty pizza box on the counter. Several guys sweep by, grabbing slices. Two of them sit down at the counter like civilized humans but the third stands right next to the box, stuffing an entire slice in his mouth while grabbing for the last slice, too.

"Okaaaay." Becky says. "Looks like the pizza's

gone."

I laugh. "Seriously. I need to go to the bathroom."

"To throw up in disgust?" she says, eyeing the guys. She pours two glasses of mineral water and hands one to me.

"No. Even though they are foul."

She rolls her eyes as two of them start arm wrestling. "You sure? It's not too late to change your mind."

It's dark in the hallway; there's a UV bulb in the overhead light. The white stripes on my tights glow as do everyone's eyes, which makes them look possessed. Anyone who's smiling has glow-in-the-dark teeth.

I can just make out the back of Sarah's head at the end of the hallway, so I make my way over to give her a hug. At the end of the hallway a sudden surge of humanity pushes her just out of reach and I swipe air. I break through the bodies and tap her on the shoulder before she disappears again. As she turns her head to see who it is, I spot Jesse over in the corner with Mike Deegan and a couple of cheerleaders.

"Indy!" Sarah is all smiles. A lopsided "Birthday Princess" tiara holds her long curls away from her face. Tommy has his arm around her waist. She's radiant from the attention. Behind her back I see Jesse watching me. "Oh my God. Monique told me what happened and I thought you weren't coming but you're here!" She gives me a hug – well, sort of. It's a half-hug at best since she doesn't detach herself from Tommy.

"Happy Birthday, Sarah," I say, trying to focus on her while still keeping an eye on Jesse.

Sarah follows my gaze. "Oh God, Indy. I'm so sorry. I didn't know he was coming. He just showed up."

I pat her on the shoulder. "It's okay. Don't worry about it."

I take a breath and square my shoulders. My river of worry is already deep enough that I'm up to my neck. What's one more thing? "Besides, after blowing him off for weeks he's probably not going to want to talk to me anyway."

She shrugs noncommittally and giggles when Tommy whispers something in her ear. "Cake outside in ten," she says with a wink. "See you out there."

Outside on the patio, giant glowing paper lanterns hang from the trees, swaying in the breeze. Strategically placed trios of fat, vanilla-scented pillar candles sit in hurricane globes. Tiny flower-shaped floating candles bob in the fountain on the side of the house and in a trough on the center of the table. A bubble machine spews bubbles out towards the tree swing, which is decorated with garlands of flowers and long trailing ribbons.

It is magical, and I wonder briefly what it would be like to have a family that would go to this much trouble for a birthday party.

We sing to Sarah, who looks like a golden goddess in the candlelight. Becky reappears by my side and I search the crowd for Monique and Austin. They stand a few feet away from Sarah. Monique waves a loose-fingered wave. She's probably dizzy from all the kissing.

Sarah squints her eyes tightly and clasps her hands together as she makes her wish. She blows, and the candles all go out. A wild cheer ensues. Hands grab for cake before the smoke has even cleared, people break off into groups to savor the sweetness in the candlelight.

Sarah hands me a slice with some of the roses. "I saved you a piece with flowers, Indy." A familiar pair of hands grabs a plated slice to my right, and Sarah's eyes go wide. "Um...okay, then, enjoy," she says, turning back to Tommy.

I turn slowly. I don't know what to say. What he'll say.

"Hey," is the only thing that comes out. *Stellar.*

"Hey yourself," he says, his expression unreadable. He glances away. "Didn't think I'd see you here tonight."

"Well, you almost didn't. If my mom finds out I'm dead."

"It's a funny thing. Not seeing you. More like a habit. How you are there one minute and then just vanish the next?"

"I know. And I'm sorry."

"Are you?" His voice is strained, the chords in his neck rippling with disapproval.

"If you'd just let me explain—"

"Why? So you can turn around and disappear again? No thanks." He turns away.

Before I can stop myself, I grab his arm. "Wait! Jesse. Please."

He turns to look at me and then I know. I've blown this one good thing. No, if I'm honest with myself I've blown all my good things and I'm standing here alone in the pile of wreckage. Everything that's happened has been my fault. A series of messed-up choices, one after another.

Not this time. Not while he's standing here living and breathing right in front of me. I have to take a chance. I have to try.

Here goes. I take a breath. "Look. You have every right to be mad. I know I haven't been fair. It's just... my life has been so messed-up for so long that I can't even think straight. I wish I could take it all back and do things differently."

"Do you?"

"Yes. Please believe me. I am such an idiot. I should have called you back. My family is falling apart and then all of a sudden I had my audition coming up. So many times I wanted to tell you what was going on but I just couldn't. I thought about it a million times but then I went to New York and..."

I am babbling. I know this, but I am powerless to stop it. My mouth churns out more words and there doesn't seem to be an off button. My hands flit a nervous little dance at my sides as I ramble on.

"...and then it felt like too much time had gone by and it was too late and I knew I should have at least said something but I—"

"Indigo. Just stop for a second."

He takes my hand and warmth zings up my arm. My feet feel rooted in place, like gravity is pressing them down with a force multiplied exponentially times ten. I gulp audibly, afraid to look at him because the feelings making my stomach flip are strong enough that I may never be the same again.

He turns me to face him and that is when it happens. I look at him, really look at him; his hair falling carelessly across his brow, the slope of his neck, the way his jeans show the curve of his thighs.

His eyes are liquid obsidian in the muted darkness that surrounds us. Hunger swims just below the surface. I know because I feel it too. I catch my breath, my heart pounding like it's trying to escape my chest.

There's a flash of a dimple as he cracks a half-smile. "You know, if you would just—" I close the space between us and press my lips to his, wrapping my arms around his broad back. My fingers find hold in his hair, and his hands cup the sides of my face. "—stop talking for a second." His voice is husky.

He pulls me in tightly, his hands caressing the back of my neck as his lips brush mine softly, teasing, then more intently. A rushing warmth turns my insides to Jell-O as heat trails down my body. We pull each other closer, wildly, as jumbled thoughts crash through my brain, crazy ideas about crushed blackberries baking in the summer sun, blue skies, and wings. This feels like flying.

Only it's not flying, but its complete opposite – falling. Plummeting towards...I don't know where. I only know I want more.

chapter twenty~six

The library parking lot is empty when I pull up. It should be, since it's Sunday morning. I can't believe Mom bought my study date excuse. The library doesn't even open for another few hours.

Another day, another lie.

I lock my bicycle and a murder of crows flies overhead, their raspy cries echoing in the surrounding stillness. I watch them fluttering across the sky, moving in unison like a corps de ballets. For them it's instinct and they don't have to earn their spot in the crowd.

At last I hear Becky's car sputtering up the driveway.

"Sorry I'm late," Becky says when I hop in. "Stupid car wouldn't start this morning. It took me like ten tries. I think I flooded the engine." She's wearing a black velvet hat, a black wool coat embroidered with blue flowers, and lacy stockings.

"What's with the outfit?" I ask. "Got a hot date later?"

"I wish. No, my mom's dragging us to some fancy luncheon later. She made me promise to dress 'like a lady.' " She air-quotes with one hand, keeping the other on the wheel.

"What does that mean?"

"I know, right? And get this – my dad took me aside and said he and my mom are concerned because they think I dress too 'outlandishly.' " Another air-quote.

"Is that even a word?"

She blows out an exasperated breath. "If it is, it's from an entirely different century. The funny thing is, I thought I was dressed pretty conservatively."

I pause before we get into the meeting hall, run my hand over the carved wooden door out front and think about the first time we came here – how strange it felt to be here. But week after week I think about the people I've met here, the things they've said that have stuck with me. Somehow they find a way to cope, even those who have it even worse than I do.

Today Rob has the floor. Everything about the man is large. His hands and feet are enormous, as is his shiny bald head. He is tall and broad with a thick, muscular neck. His upper arms are the size of my thighs. His presence is mesmerizing, made even more so by his smooth, dark skin and booming voice.

"I kept thinking it was my fault. But then I realized she makes bad choices." When Rob speaks, every word he says is spoken carefully, deliberately. It's easy to follow and you hang on every word.

"I've been doing a lot of reading about detachment lately. I realize I play my part too, every time I try to rescue, save or fix her. I decided it's time to try something different, to allow her to falter and fail and not be led by guilt to feel responsible for that faltering and failure. If I stop bailing her out then she will have to accept personal responsibility for her actions. Maybe it's time to back away. I have to put myself first – not hang on beyond a reasonable and rational point." His voice breaks and he looks away, taking a deep breath.

"There's a difference between who she really is and who I want her to be. It's time for me to accept that, put my well-being first and distance myself from a hurtful relationship that I can neither control nor change."

Later we all gather around the coffee area. I pour myself a half-cup, watching the stream of dark liquid and notice my matching dark thoughts.

Bella stands to my right, stirring cream into her cup. She's in flowy black layers today. A beautiful silver and turquoise squash blossom necklace shimmers at her throat. She lays a hand on my shoulder. "How you doin', kiddo? You look a little glum today."

"Okay, I guess."

She smiles gently. "One of those days, huh?"

"I always feel this push-pull when I come here; I agree with what people say but I'm not sure how to apply it to my life. Or if it would even work."

"It's a process, you know? You tinker a little bit here and there until you find what works. One thing's for sure – keep doing the same and you get more of the same."

Even though I know she's right this doesn't make me feel better. "I suppose."

She looks pensive for a moment. "You know, Indigo, it's like the butterfly effect. Have you heard of it? The idea that the movement of a butterfly's wings – something so small and insignificant – creates a ripple effect that creates huge change elsewhere. That's what we are, you and me. The wings of change."

I find Becky over in the corner talking animatedly with Rob. I don't want to interrupt their conversation, and all I can think about right now is lying down somewhere quiet. I stand off to the side and wait. Minutes tick by and the itchy feeling worsens. I may as well be invisible. I amuse myself by reading the CPR poster on the wall. Except there's nothing amusing about saving choking victims.

"Indigo." Rob has somehow detached himself from his conversation with Becky. "How are you?"

"I'm okay."

"No, really. How are you?"

I sigh. "You know what, Rob? I'm tired. I'm really, really tired."

"I know that feeling. Go on."

"It's like there's this huge wall and I keep conking my head on it."

"There's always a way around that wall. You go over it, around it, or maybe even through it. But you need your people. The ones who have your back, the ones you can trust."

Who are they? Where are they? That's what I want to say to him, but the concern in his eyes stops me. He squeezes my hand and says, "You'll be all right. I can just tell. You've got a backbone, girl."

Becky waves for my attention from her spot at the front door. She points at her watch. Which is completely ironic and unbelievably refreshing for a change.

"See you, Rob."

"You know it," he says with a laugh.

Back at the library, Becky parks and cuts the engine. "You're sure you'll be all right? Should I call you later?"

"I'm fine." I climb out and sling my backpack on my shoulder.

The window rolls down. "Because I can totally

check in with you. Whenever you need—"

"Just go," I say, waving her off. "I'll be fine. Seriously."

"Okay, 'cause I just—"

I roll my eyes and raise my palms in a gesture of supplication. "Go forth, you and your fancy tights. I'll talk to you later."

She grins and starts the engine. On the first try. I watch her drive away until she's a mottled speck in the distance.

I get on my bike and think about "my people"… and growing some wings.

I study the back door in our garage. If I'm completely honest with myself, I don't feel like opening the door and going inside. But I can't keep staring at its glossy black surface and my pale, ghostlike reflection.

When I open the back door, Brad and Charlie are mid-argument. As usual.

Brad: "Charlie, you didn't flush."

Charlie: "Yes, I did."

Brad: "Dude. You didn't. Now it stinks in there. There was a giant turd floating in the bowl."

Charlie: "Your poop stinks too! You stink!"

Five minutes later.

Brad: "You have to put the controllers away."

Charlie: "I did put them away."

Brad: "You have to wind up the cords. You just threw them in the box."

Charlie: "I did wind the cords."

Brad: "Yeah, right."

They continue lobbing insults. It's like watching tennis at super close range, and it's making me dizzy.

Mom marches by and her footsteps retreat to the laundry room. Wham! The washing machine door slams shut. I hear the clink of a bottle and the sound of her plastic cup hitting the counter a few seconds later. Great. She's already pounding shots.

Her footsteps thump back through the kitchen.

She stands in the doorway, glaring at us, a mound of laundry in her arms. "Goddamn it to hell! Haven't I told you a million times to turn your clothes right side out? For crying out loud, I am not your servant." She throws the heap of clothes on the floor in front of her. "Get off your lazy butts and turn them the right way out! Now!!"

My brothers meekly slither over to the laundry pile. Brad eyes it before he bends down to deal with it. They sort through the clothes and Brad carries the pile back to the laundry room.

When he returns, our eyes meet. "Outside," Brad says. No argument from Charlie or me.

It's our unspoken rule to stay out of sight and avoid Mom whenever she's in a foul mood. An hour or two from now it will blow over.

I halfheartedly throw the basketball. I don't feel like being out here right now. Brad shoots a few ridiculously epic shots, one with his back turned. We always give Charlie handicap points because he's so little. Today we even let him win.

"I want to jump," Charlie says. He's flushed with victory. Brad and I take an end of the jump rope and swing it for him. I stifle a laugh; he has this totally discombobulated way of jumping. He raises his knees so high they're almost tucked into his chest and his hair flies up and down like a bad toupee.

"Dude, you need to put some product in that hair," Brad says. "It's all over the place." This from the guy who walks around with major bed head half the time.

Charlie stops jumping. He bites his lip and crosses his legs. His body says it needs to go to the bathroom but his mind either hasn't caught on yet or doesn't want to obey because playing is so much more fun.

Brad catches on too, but we both play it cool. If we call attention to it, Charlie will deny it.

Five minutes later the light bulb goes on. Charlie looks desperate. "I gotta pee."

"Well, no one's stopping you. Go on. But hurry back outside when you're done." I watch him disappear through the back door. "Let's hope he makes it in time," I say to Brad.

Then I remember something. Charlie went in there by himself. One of us should have gone with him. I grab my water bottle and run to the house. Just as I'm on the stairs, my hand on the door handle, I hear it. A crash. Charlie screams.

"God-fucking-dammit!" Mom roars. "You little shit! You asshole! THAT IS IT!! I've had it with you!"

More crashes. Charlie screams. A slap, followed by wailing.

Get in there, Indigo. Help him. Now. The voice inside my head is calm yet firm. As soon as the words go through my mind, an electric jolt moves my hand back into action. *Yes. GO. You have to help him.*

Yanking the back door open, I stumble over the threshold. Shards of glass and juice litter the kitchen floor. My mother and Charlie stand in the lake of orange juice in the middle of the floor. Her back is to me, so I can't see her face. All I see are her hands – wrapped around my brother's neck.

She shakes him violently back and forth. "You little—" she snarls. Her guttural growl is beastly, far beyond any sense of conscience or control.

My brother's face is turning blue.

"Mom!" I scream. "Mom! Let him go!"

She doesn't hear me. She doesn't stop. I have to get through to her. I have to break the spell.

"Mom! MOM!!" I scream but she doesn't let go. Charlie's face is terrible. The shade of blue is deepening.

I lunge at her, grab her hands. Nothing. I claw at her and scream from the roots of my being, like my guts are being ripped inside out. "MOM!! WAKE UP!! LET

HIM GO!! YOU'RE KILLING HIM!" I grab her wrists and dig my nails into the flesh. I clamp them in and pull.

A final tug and he is free.

She whirls, her eyes still glazed over with madness. I hardly recognize her at all. Behind her, Charlie coughs uncontrollably. Color blooms in his cheeks. She blinks. Clarity flickers in her eyes.

Our eyes lock together. If I had fur, it would be standing straight up my back. I'm crouched, ready to pounce again if I need to.

She's crossed a line and we both know it. The white wall behind her blazes with a ghostly, silvery imprint of her outline, like the negative image of her last actions living on.

Only this one won't ever fade away. I'm sure of it.

The clock in the pantry ticks loudly, the only witness to all of this. Each tick crashes through the space between us like a sledgehammer. Boom.

I hear Charlie's dim sobs in the background. The glare of wrongness hovers in the air around us. We don't move. Like someone tuned off the music in a game of freeze-dance.

She draws herself up tall, like she's taking back her power, reminding us all that she is in control. But we both know better. She looks at me. Does she hate herself more than I do right now?

"Fine. He's your responsibility now," she hisses. "Keep him out of my sight."

chapter twenty-seven

I dial and hear the phone ring on the other end. I feel a flash of guilt about calling people this early on Sunday morning but I don't have a choice. It's time to mobilize the forces. My people.

The irony that today is supposed to be "family day" is beyond ludicrous.

"Can you come now?" I say. The voice on the other end responds affirmatively. I hang up quickly and look at Brad.

"That's the last one," I tell him.

He nods. "Now what?"

"Now we wait."

Wait and hope.

"Everyone needs to be here before Dad gets back

from the store." I pace while I go over my mental checklist one last time. So far Mom hasn't even gotten out of bed yet today. That's one thing that's working for us.

"How's Mom?" Brad asks.

"When I brought her juice and toast an hour ago, she was really quiet and pale. Her hands were shaking. I think she's so freaked out that she's going cold turkey."

There's a quiet knock at the back door. I open it and relax a little when I see Mrs. Rusch's large, comforting form. Her eyes look big and sad through the thick lenses of her glasses. She hugs me and I already feel stronger, like we can deal with what lies ahead.

"Oh, honey, I'm so sorry for all you've been through," she says. "I knew something wasn't right. I'm really glad you called me. We're going to set things straight; I just know it."

I lead Mrs. Rusch to the living room. "You man the back door now," I tell Brad.

"On it. Hey, Mrs. Rusch." Brad's job is to get everyone else inside as stealthily as possible. I will prep everyone in the living room as they arrive. Charlie is watching a movie upstairs; we built a special fort on his bottom bunk. Hopefully he'll stay there.

A short while later the entire party is here: my mom's two closest friends, Mrs. Rusch and Mrs. Haig, Miss Roberta, and Mr. Johnstone, my dad's best friend since childhood. It hits me that this is the first time we've had so many visitors in a long time. My parents never entertain anymore.

Everyone speaks in whispers. Tight smiles and nervous glances fly around the room. It's like the last few moments just before a surprise party – minus the party – although there will be a surprise.

A car door slams, followed by a short beep. Dad comes in whistling, an indication that he's in a good mood. The whistling stops the minute he strolls into the living room and sees everyone sitting there. "Uh – hello everyone. No one told me we were having a party today. Did I miss a memo or something?"

"No, Jake, you didn't," Mr. Johnstone says quietly. "We came here to talk to you about something. A problem that needs to be dealt with."

"What do you mean, Eric?" Dad looks confused. "Is everything all right?"

"No, Jake, it isn't, and I think you know that," Mrs. Rusch adds. My dad looks at her like she has six heads.

"Lissie's drinking is out of control, Jake," Mr. Johnstone continues.

"What? Oh come on, Brad, it's not like you and I haven't tied one on before."

"It isn't like that. Not anymore."

Dad laughs nervously, like he's hoping it's all a joke. "Look, I appreciate everyone's concern but I think you have it all wrong. Everything here is under control —"

"No, Jake. It isn't," Mrs. Rausch says.

Mr. Johnstone puts a hand on Dad's shoulder.

"Jake. Indigo called us all because she's very worried. Are you aware of Lissie's behavior yesterday? Tell him what happened, Indigo."

This time my dad is forced to hear me out without interrupting; no one here will let him try to pretend this away. Knowing this makes it easier to talk about what happened, even though the details are so ugly. It's like I've finally found my voice in the company of all of these people.

My people.

"Oh, Christ," he says when I finish. He runs his hands through his hair and clutches his head, staring morosely down at the floor. Hi shoulders sag. "How can this be happening?"

Miss Roberta clears her throat. "You understand the severity of the situation, Jake. We need to act."

"Yes, yes. Okay. Got any ideas?" Dad says, looking wildly around the room.

"Actually, yes. We do."

Mom lies in bed reading quietly. She's a shrunken version of her usual self. She looks up from her book as we arrive one by one. Her face works through a series of expressions: confusion, surprise, wariness. Her eyes narrow in defense. With a slight shake of her head, she forces herself into composure.

"Wow, what a surprise you all. What's everyone doing here?" The Christmas voice is back in full swing, with just a hint of a Southern drawl.

But this time it won't work.

She's not going to give up without a fight, though. I can tell by way she sets her shoulders. Her hands clench the sides of her (romance) novel protectively. She sits up a little bit taller against the pillows and looks at us defiantly.

Mrs. Haig approaches the foot of the bed. "Lissie, we're here because we're worried about you." She puts her hand gently on the end of the bed. "You have a problem, Lissie, and we want to help you."

Mom laughs it off. "Now, Claire, I'm just not feeling well today is all. I'm going to be fine. I appreciate you coming over today, really I do, but—"

"Look, Lissie, I am not going to stand by and pretend anything's fine any longer. I just can't. I couldn't live with myself, knowing what I know. You are my friend – I care about you. But you have a problem with alcohol. Whether you're able to admit it or not, it's the truth. I'm here to help you and your family and to get you the treatment you need. Will you let us help you?"

"*No.*" My mother instantly degenerates into a small child. "No, no, no." Her lower lip juts out. She crosses her arms and stares at a spot in front of her.

"Mom," Brad pipes in, "you can't hide it anymore. We know everything. We can't do this anymore, Mom.

Please. You have to get treatment."

I piggyback on Brad's comments. "He's right, Mom. You aren't in control of it anymore; it's controlling you. After what happened yesterday can you honestly say that you are okay?" I look her square in the eye. "You need help. Please say yes."

Mrs. Rusch and Miss Roberta both start talking at once. Mrs. Rusch continues. "I've known you for a long time, Lissie, and I've known something was wrong for awhile. I just didn't know what, since you never told me. But now that I know, I want to help you. If you look around this room, I think you will see that it is filled with people who love you and want the best for you. It's that simple. Please let us help you."

Miss Roberta glances around before saying her piece. "Lissie, you work hard to give your family the best. But some problems are bigger than us. They are simply too heavy to hold by yourself. We won't let you fall."

"Liss—" my dad says softly. "We need you. But not like this. Say yes to help and our family. Please say yes."

My mother shakes her head. "I can't believe this. All of you – I don't want this."

I step forward. "Mom, you need help. You need to do this. If you don't—" I look at Brad and he nods, "—I will call the police and tell them everything."

My mother stares at her lap for a long time. She grabs the cup of juice with visibly trembling hands, takes a sip and sets it down again. "All right," she says in a tiny, soft voice. "I'll go."

Later that night I lie in bed with the lights off and something stirs in my chest, a sparkly, fluttery thing. Like the darkness is finally receding.

Behind my eyelids I see faces: Becky, Miss Roberta, Mrs. Haig, Mrs. Rusch, Bella, and a few of the people from our support group. The faces fill the vision, overlapping one another, until they melt into a kaleidoscope of color and dissolve into points of light, glowing softly in the surrounding darkness, the edges of each one bleeding into the edge of the next.

But there's a stronger glow – a pillar of light that runs right through my core. It's what gave me the strength to do what I've had to do: to say no. Even when it meant saying no to my own mother.

I realize that even in the darkest moments, light is still there. You just have to look for it.

Even though I don't know what the future will look like, at least it will be different from now on.

chapter twenty-eight

Brad, Charlie and I stand huddled in the driveway watching Dad load Mom's suitcase into the car. She follows in her fuchsia velour warm-ups. The color defies the heavy mood surrounding us all. She looks hunched and wrinkled, like she's aged ten years overnight. Dad walks like he's carrying a million pounds.

I know what he's going through. I know all about the worry, anger, resentment and fear balled up together in the pit of your stomach like a lead weight. We're traveling the same road; I'm just a little farther ahead. Now he's also got to keep our household running while my mom is getting treatment. I don't envy him.

My mother gives hugs on her way to the car. I give her a half-hearted hug; it's all I can do not to turn and walk away. The tangle in my stomach reminds me that although she's going for treatment, there's no guarantee she'll recover and stay sober.

She stoops to hug Charlie and he stiffens in her embrace. When she releases him he runs over to me. I don't blame him. Maybe he's young enough that he'll forget everything in a few days.

I sigh. In a way, my worst fear has come to pass. Mom will disappear, at least temporarily. Things are already different, already changing, and we don't know what lies ahead. It helps to know that we aren't alone, that there are people who care and who are willing to help.

My brothers and I stand in place, even after the car disappears down the driveway.

"Will Mom get better, Indy?" Charlie asks.

"I don't know. I hope so," I say. But I think, *I'm glad she's going away. I feel like I can breathe again.*

For now, there's peace, and that's enough.

Later that morning during ballet class I can't stop thinking about the studio at the New York School of Ballet. During pliés I remember the wide expanse of perfect, grey flooring, the three levels of barres attached to the wall, the perfect white interior and the glossy black grand piano. Thankfully I don't think of Mom at all for a change. Instead I miss having a real, live pianist during class. By the time we move to the floor I ache to return to New York.

Out in the center I watch myself in the mirror during tendus and feel a funny uneasiness in my solar plexus. I wonder why, now that Mom is finally getting help. When we practice piqué turns on the diagonal, I push myself harder, whipping off double turns. Then I know why my stomach hurts: dread that I won't return to New York. I feel another wave of disappointment and I don't know what to do about it.

When class ends, I hang back to practice the turning sequence. I keep running through it until the sweat pours down my back and my face turns red from exertion.

Miss Roberta appraises me. "Something's happened to you, Indigo," she says. "I've noticed it ever since you went to New York."

I freeze. She knows everything…how I'm not going to get in to NYSB, how much of a mess I am, and about Jesse.

She gives me another appraising look. "I think I know what it is."

I lose about three inches in height as I deflate under her gaze.

"I know exactly what it is because the same thing happened to me." She points a finger. "Just like you, I went and fell in love."

I knew it. She freaking knows.

"It's not something you can explain with words. It's just something you feel. A fire. An unquenchable fire. And the only thing that can put out the flames is more of the same." She pauses. "Does that make sense to you?"

"I think so," I admit quietly.

"So then I'm right – you have been bitten by the bug. Once you get a taste of life at New York School of Ballet you are never quite the same."

I look at her, confused. I'm no longer sure what we're talking about.

"I see it in you, Indigo, the same way I felt it in my blood when it happened to me. It was magical…that world. Once I was there I couldn't imagine life without it. I realized I was willing to work relentlessly, do whatever I had to, to have that life."

I look at the floor. At her feet. She has it all wrong. She has no idea that I've failed.

"But Miss Roberta—"

"You have that drive, Indigo. I know you do. Even though life has been difficult lately, I still see you showing up. Still see you pushing yourself."

"It's not enough, Miss Roberta."

"What do you mean, not enough?"

I tell her everything. Well, almost. I leave out the part about Jesse. That would push her over the edge.

"Well," she says. She taps her chin with a finger. "You never know what will happen until you get that letter in the mail. Who knows? You might have made a better impression than you think." She laughs. "They'll certainly remember you." She touches my arm. "So we'll just see. Until then, we work. And if it isn't a yes this year, then we work until it is a yes. As I told you before, Indigo, the choice is always yours. You have to decide how badly you want it."

When I leave the studio the sky is the bluest it's been in months. I watch shapes in the clouds while I wait for Dad to pick me up. I feel the irresistible urge to spin in the grass like I did when I was a kid.

My heart skips with a new lightness. Maybe there's hope after all, time to make my dream happen.

One way or another.

The late afternoon sun is warm on my back and the wind whips my hair around. I run holding Jesse's hand and it feels like flying, especially if I close my eyes. There's a sense of freedom in letting go because I trust him.

I trust him. I can't say that about many people. But there is an innate goodness inside of him, a palpable thing. Is it possible to feel the pureness of a person's heart? I think it must be. Because every time I get near him I feel calm. Okay, not calm, exactly. It's not really possible to be calm and turned on at the same time. So it isn't that.

He squeezes me tightly against his body, as if he senses my thoughts. We walk on and little bursts of scents drift by: daffodils, dogwoods, and freshly-mown grass. My favorite signs of spring.

Myer's Bridge is quiet, peaceful, and private. So unlike home. But today it feels like home, or how home ought to be. The water is silvery still, like mercury. Weeping willows line the shoreline, their sad leaves trailing inches above the water. Several ducks swim over, hoping for a handout. When I was little, Mom often took us here to give out the ends of our bread loaves.

Jesse grabs my hand, pulling me into a run down the trail. The tall reeds whisper across my legs.

"Stop, you," I say, laughing. "I don't want to end up on my butt."

He skids ahead of me down a treacherous bit and turns to offer me his hand. I grab it and leap down next to him.

"A bold maneuver by the inestimable Indigo Stevens," he says in his best cheesy ringmaster's impression.

"Have I told you you're a goof?"

"That's part of the reason you like me," he says, stealing a kiss.

We walk along the water's edge and find a seat in the tall grass that lines the shore.

"You're too far away," he says. "C'mere."

I scoot over next to him and keep scooting until he

falls over. I quickly wrestle him to the ground, pinning his arms overhead. "Is this close enough for you?" I ask wickedly.

"Almost."

I lower my head and kiss him again, long and deep. "How about now?"

"Just about."

I bend my head again. His lips are soft, like summer fruit. Warmth floods my body and I feel the tug of wanting. Wanting all of him. The driving desire to line up every one of my cells with every one of his. Must. Stop. I pull away.

Our eyes stay connected. Breathing heavy, I swallow, trying to regain composure. "Now that you are in my clutches, I think I'll—"

He rolls, pinning me to the ground. "You were saying?" he says, breathing heavily.

"That was—"

He cuts me off again, his lips back on mine. Must stop kissing him. This is dangerous ground and we both know it. But it feels so delicious. The weight of his body, his strong thighs…

I pull my hands free and cradle his face. I kiss him deeply, not holding anything back. Then I wriggle free, jump to my feet and take off running through the reeds.

"Diabolical move!" He laughs as he struggles back to his feet.

I run ahead, but hear his feet pounding down the trail after me. His arm snakes around my waist moments later. He pulls me in tightly against his body, then spins me around to face him.

"I think we belong together. What do you think?" He says, gently brushing a stray lock of hair off my neck. His eyes are serious.

"I—" My breath catches in my throat. I look at him, the power of his emotions painted across the planes of his face, and I think about everything Miss Roberta said today. And then I know. *I am leading you on.* I can't give myself to him. Not really. Ballet will always come first.

Tears burn, threatening to spill in torrents if I don't rein them in immediately. I can't look at him, so I bury my head in his neck. "I love being with you," I mumble into his neck.

I feel his arms around me, our bodies wound tightly together, feel the beating of his heart echoing my own and hear the bubbly currents at the shoreline, the whispers of the reeds, birds trilling overhead.

While I'm aware of these things around us, they feel distant, separate, more muted. They are the background, the stage.

A cloud passes over the sun, stealing the light, like a curtain coming down at the end of a performance. And just like that, a shadow passes over my heart with the thought that this may all be temporary. I've cast my wish out into the world and forces are at work, even now, to make that dream come true.

And if that's the case, none of this may last.

chapter twenty-nine

The wrought-iron gates at the entrance of Silver Hills are from another time, the era of grand estates. The long driveway winds over grassy rolling hills, past a pond full of ducks and geese paddling around. The driveway ends near a large white house with forest-green shutters.

"Why do we have to go to this again?" Brad moans from the backseat of the car.

"Because," Dad says, eying Brad in the rearview mirror, "we all need to learn new patterns of behavior if we want our family to heal."

Charlie reads in the seat next to me, happily oblivious to everything. There's a pile of books on the seat beside him. I have to laugh; the drive to Silver

Hills only takes twenty minutes and he's packed enough reading material to last several days.

I envy his ability to lose himself in literature. I don't know what to expect from this visit with Mom. If this is his way of coping with nervous angst, then he's one step ahead of the game. My technique: roll down the window for some fresh air. Check out the view. Breathe.

"Posh," Brad declares as we climb the brick steps to the front door. "This place is huge. It must have, what, like ten bedrooms?"

"They can accommodate ten residents in the main house and more in the private cottages out back," Dad replies.

"Creepy gothic," Brad says, squinting up at the roof. "Look at that weird little window on the top floor. You think they send the problem cases up there?"

"It was a hotel back in the day," Dad says, pointedly ignoring Brad. "Word is that it was quite the place to be seen."

The entry hall is warm and bright, filled with the scent of lavender. A few rows of chairs are set up in the salon to our right, and several people have already claimed seats.

"Let's sit together in the back," Dad suggests. "That way if we need to make a restroom run we won't disturb anybody." He turns to Charlie. "Let's swing through there now."

They disappear down the hall, leaving Brad and I

standing here. It's dead silent in the room except for the occasional squeak and groan of chairs as people shift in their seats. Getting comfortable in metal folding chairs is impossible. We grab seats in the back and wait. I check out people's shoes on the sly, a technique I developed when I was five and bored in church.

Burgundy heels, pretty hot. Loafers with tassels, eeewwww. Puce ballet flats, kinda cute except for the horrid color. Hush Puppies, or something equally repulsive, pass by my field of vision. They are attached to a man in khaki pants and a navy blue sport coat. He approaches the front of the room.

"Good morning, everyone, and welcome. I'm Robert Witherspoon, the director here at Silver Hills."

I stifle a yawn. I could go the rest of my life without formal presentations. Especially from people who voluntarily wear the unofficial men's East Coast preppy uniform like Mr. Witherspoon. My brothers each have the same khaki/navy ensemble hanging in their closets in their respective sizes.

History of the place, what they do here now (as if we didn't already know), what the day is about. Blah, blah, blah. I stifle another yawn. The lady in front of me blows her nose so loudly it trumpets.

"But enough background. Let's get to the meat of the matter." Mr. Witherspoon is obviously not a vegetarian. "Journaling is an important part of the healing process for our residents. They journal every day and we recommend the same for everyone in this room. I'd like to share a few entries with you to illustrate my point."

He aims a controller at the projector in the back of the room and an image beams on the wall behind him. The handwriting of this journal entry is loopy script that's hard to decipher. He reads it aloud:

"I want to start over. Live my life differently. I realize I have choices. If I want a different life, I need to make different choices."

He clicks to the next image. Bold, block letters fill the screen. *"I am an alcoholic, but I'm also many other things. I'm a father, a husband, a brother and a lawyer. My family is the most important part of my life and I want to be a healthy part of it. Today I'm choosing to put my family first."*

The next image is writing I'd know anywhere. After years of permission slips, class signups and checks, my mother's cursive is almost as familiar as my own – and virtually impossible to copy. Not that I've tried. She has her own strange blend of cursive print: bold, loopy flourishes interlaced with tiny, neat patches.

"I hate this disease. I hate what it's done to my life and to my family. But I refuse to give up. I won't let it win. I'm going to fight."

I want to believe those words. But I'm not sure she has it in her.

Mr. Witherspoon clicks a button and the projector goes dark. "As I've said, journaling is a powerful tool of expression. We've found it helpful for everyone we work with. Now it's your turn."

He passes out pale blue thin composition books and pens. "Take your time. There is no required length, no right or wrong way to answer. Think of it as an experiment."

He clears his throat again. "Here are a few questions to consider: what are your fears about having your family member come home from treatment? What are your hopes? What do you need to have a fresh start?"

This feels suspiciously like school. Brad crosses his eyes at me when I look his way. I suppress a laugh and force myself to cough, disguising it. Most of the other people scribble furiously; the rasping sound of their pens connecting across the pages breaks the silence. I sit and will the words to come. I know what my hopes and fears are. But what I would need to move on? What it would take to forgive? Nothing comes. The blank paper stares at me accusingly. This is a joke.

I write: *I am afraid that my mother will slip back into old patterns. I'm not sure she is able to change. I'm afraid of dealing with her mood swings and her unpredictable fits of rage. I don't even know how to begin to forgive her and I don't know if I ever will.*

My hopes? *I hope she gets what she needs. I hope life at home will be peaceful. Most of all, I hope for a mother who isn't angry all the time.*

I need two things to be able to move on: I need her to admit how unfair she has been. I need her to tell me that she is sorry and will do everything in her power to stay sober.

When I read my entry, I'm surprised. It's as if the words on the page came from somewhere else.

Can these things ever happen?

The room brightens as sun streams through the windows. Maybe it's a sign of brighter things to come.

"You may be surprised by your answers. Sometimes writing helps us access deeper parts of ourselves that are hidden below the surface. We recommend discussing these answers as a family at some point before your family member returns home. It's part of the plan to help families reunify. Every person who participates in our program learns to expect to have this conversation, since forgiveness and making amends are a huge piece of long-term success.

"Recovery brings up a lot of feelings for everyone. For some it is hard to trust that the alcoholic will change. If you are unable to believe, aim to temporarily suspend disbelief and keep an open mind.

"We have additional materials for you to take home. There are flyers for some of our workshops and a list of resources for you and your family.

"I'm sure you are all anxious to get on with visiting. We have set up some refreshments outside on the patio. Your family members will meet you there."

The outdoor tables overlook a garden filled with a sea of color. The crisp, white umbrellas and starched linen tablecloths make it look like a fancy restaurant.

The air is laden with the sweet smell of honeysuckle and rose.

Charlie spots Mom first, and goes running over to her. How quickly he forgets what she's done. He's good at moving on. Even though I'm glad to see he's happy, I look at Mom's hands rubbing his back and feel my breath quicken as I have a sudden flashback.

I blink the vision away and force myself to look at something else. Mom's shoes. Her delicately-beaded silver sandals show off her perfect pedicure. Hot pink nail polish, like Miami flamingos on hyper-drive. I hug her stiffly and walk away.

Get a hold of yourself, Indigo. If I can't deal with a quick visit, how will I live under the same roof with the woman? I proceed to the refreshment table, refilling my glass several times to delay going back. Plus, they've added strawberries to the lemonade so it's extra delicious.

I return with lemonades for everyone. I look at my family sipping the sweet beverage in this perfect setting. If someone were to snap a picture of us right now, we would look like a normal, healthy family.

Except for the awkward silence.

"Why don't I show you my room," Mom suggests. "Indigo, I think you will especially like it."

Can't imagine why. "Sure, Mom."

Charlie holds her hand. Traitor.

Her room is bright and airy. A white eyelet spread covers the bed, and matching curtains hang in the windows. A slight breeze ruffles the edges of the curtains like someone just walked by.

My eyes rove the walls, settling on tiny watercolor still-life paintings hanging over the desk. They are the only splashes of color in the entire room, and I move in to get a better look. I'm shocked to see Mom's name scrawled in the lower right corner. I didn't know she could paint. Being here feels like invading her space.

"I didn't even know I could paint," she says, like she's reading my mind. Maybe she can – some weird mom superpower. She laughs nervously. "That was a surprise, and not the only one since I got here, believe me."

"They're good, Mom," I offer.

"Thanks. The colors are cheerful. That helps. Otherwise this place is too white. Feels clinical, you know?"

"Your room is nice, Mom," Charlie says.

"Come see my little deck."

Charlie, Brad, and Dad follow her out the French doors into the sunshine, but it looks crowded enough with the four of them, so I hang back. The desk is littered with pages of things she's written. A journal? Letters? I start reading before I can stop myself.

Pale blue light,
Tick tock beating,
The heart of an eyeless face
Sole sentry over heavy-eyed dreamers
In a wink, an eye

The spell is broken
Morning bleeds in

She's writing poetry. Yet another one of her hidden secrets, another chamber she's locked away. I have lived with her for almost sixteen years and I've never seen her write anything besides grocery lists and calendar items.

This split between the version of Mom I know and the person she really is gives me an uneasy, eerie feeling, like the Earth is tilting and bobbing on its axis.

She's Mom. She is—

I don't know who she is anymore.

chapter Thirty

The clock on my bedside table reads 5:55 am in glowing red numbers. I swallow a groan. I have this rule: never get up before 6:00 am. But today I have to; today Mom comes home. At least there is actual daylight gleaming under the edge of the window shade. Getting up in the dark is unnatural and inhumane.

I tug on the shade and it flutters open. There's a flash of red. Our resident house finch is back again, just like every spring since he first appeared three years ago. His head is red with a coral undertone, unapologetically vibrant. Why is it that male birds are the pretty ones?

Of course, there are some beautiful *human* boys, too. Like Jesse.

I sit at my desk and fire up the printer. I only have a few minutes to make final corrections to my geography report before I print it out. It has to be perfect; it counts for 30% of our final grade and Lowry almost never gives out As. Her motto is, "If it's average work, which most of it will be, you'll get an average grade – which is a C." I also have to give a five-minute oral presentation. I hate giving speeches. My hands always shake and my voice sounds weird. I can dance in front of hundreds of people but I'm nervous in front of a small group of my peers. Probably because I can see their faces.

But the pit in my stomach is really about something else. *Mom comes home today.* Dad is picking her up while we're at school. I keep telling myself but it doesn't feel real.

I don't know how to feel or what to expect. It's been so peaceful around here on the one hand, but—

"Brad! Open up! I gotta go!" Charlie screeches.

"Go use Indigo's. I need to shower now or I'll be late!"

Okay, scratch peaceful. There is no such thing as peaceful around here.

Charlie comes flying through my door. "Indy, I gotta—"

"Just go. No explanations necessary."

He runs off to my bathroom and slams the door.

I start printing my report while I throw on a black pleated mini skirt and my favorite t-shirt with the curvy snakes.

I hear the toilet flushing repeatedly – not a good

sign. When I enter my bathroom, the toilet is clogged and the sink is close to overflowing since Charlie has the water on full blast while he washes his hands. My towel is on the floor with his dirty footprints all over it.

"Charlie, I can't believe you." I pick up the towel and throw it in the laundry hamper. "How can you make such a huge mess in two minutes?"

"Sorry, Indy." His lower lip sags in remorse.

"Fine. Just finish up and go. I've got to get ready for school." I stalk off, shaking my head. How can one kid be so messy?

I sit at the vanity and notice the time. Where did it go? Dealing with hallway drama and bathroom mayhem, I guess. Today is going to be a full day – the kind where one activity blurs right into the next with no downtime in between. Maybe that's a good thing; it will keep my mind off thinking about Mom too much.

But I have to put my hair up in a bun. I won't have time to do it later. I quickly bend over at the waist and dangle my head toward the floor, using gravity to get my hair up in a ponytail. A dab of lip gloss, a few strokes of purple mascara, and—

"Indy, do you think Mom will be happy when she comes home?"

"Charlie. I'm trying to get ready here. I don't know, okay?"

"But what if she's not?"

"Jesus, Charlie! I don't know! God!" I throw my brush in the drawer and slam it shut.

I sound just like her. My hands tremble as I hold my head in my hands. I stare at my lap, hating myself. Hating her. Because there are no simple answers. No promises. And that totally sucks.

I look at Charlie in the mirror. His little shoulders shake with silent sobs and I feel nauseous because I am such a horrid excuse for a human being.

"Charlie?" I say softly, but he won't look at me. "I'm sorry I got mad. It's just…we're all scared. We don't know what to expect and that's the truth. There aren't any promises. We just have to hope Mom will get better."

But what if she doesn't? The question that hangs over my head like a completely unwelcome cartoon bubble. It's not a question I want to ask myself right now. What's the point?

I pull him close to me for a hug and smell his little kid smell, part peanut butter, part sunshine. "Let's hope for the best for now, okay?"

"K. But I'm still scared."

So am I. But I'll never let him know that. Someone has to be strong for him. "I know, big guy. But you've got me and Dad and Brad to help."

The corners of his mouth droop with uncertainty.

"And Mrs. Rusch, and Miss Roberta…we've got a whole team of helpers." I'm reminding myself as much as him.

I grab my report from the printer. "Why don't you make a card for her? I bet she'd love that." I hand him an extra sheet of paper and he's off.

I shove the report in a folder and put it in my backpack, then load my dance bag for ballet class: tights, leotard and legwarmers, warm-up clothes, pointe shoes…damn. I was supposed to sew ribbons on my new pair of pointe shoes but I didn't get around to it. I throw in my sewing kit. Maybe I'll find some time during lunch.

Breakfast today actually looks edible. Dad learned how to make hard-boiled eggs. He eyes my outfit. "Going for the punk look today, are we?" Dad says as he pours orange juice for everyone.

"No. It's just comfortable," I say as I calmly peel a banana. I throw in a piece of toast, then cover it with peanut butter and top it all with sliced banana.

"Gross," Brad says when he sees my plate.

"This is nutritional perfection, the breakfast of champions, man. It's got protein and carbs for good energy and potassium. What more do you need?"

"Whatever. It's still gross."

"Yours is but one opinion," I say, popping the last bite in my mouth. "Later, y'all."

Today I will get to school on time. My bike may not be anything fancy, but it is my ticket to freedom. No relying on anyone else for transportation.

The sun feels warm on my skin as I ride. Birds call for mates. It's as if everything has come alive in the past few weeks while I've been in the studio or had my head buried in books studying for exams.

The halls at school are mostly empty when I arrive. My dance bag refuses to fit in my locker without a fight. I push it with the heels of my hands, forcing it in.

Lips brush the back of my neck, sending chills to my extremities.

Jesse follows the contour of my neck with his lips. "You. Look. Amazing," he breathes in my ear. "How about a study date tonight?"

"Can't. I've got ballet class and then a family dinner." I still haven't told him about Mom. I've spent so much of my energy dealing with her problems that I just didn't want to give away any more. I want to keep this thing with Jesse separate. Something that's just mine.

"All right…lunch?" He flutters his eyelashes.

"Sold, to the man with the fluttery eyelashes."

We celebrate Mom's return home with pizza from Tomato Joe's. We always go there because the food is delicious and Matt, the owner, always hands out slices of mozzarella while we're waiting at the pickup counter.

Dad comes in with two pizza boxes. "There are two kinds tonight: pepperoni with veggie, and mushroom with black olive," he says. "Plus we've got salad." His voice sounds jovial and forced. He glances nervously at Mom, not sure whether to let her serve or do it himself.

"I call wedges." Brad eyes the pizza and rubs his hands.

The pizza from Tomato Joe's is sliced into squares, leaving four tiny triangular wedges in every pie. This leads to sibling rivalry every time.

"You had them last time. It's my turn!" Charlie shrieks.

"Your memory sucks. You had them last time."

Dad rolls his eyes. "I'll settle this. Indigo and your mother will share them this time."

"But Dad—" both boys protest simultaneously.

"And that's final."

Mom looks at me blankly. It's weird to have her sitting across the table again. In some ways it's like she never left. But then I remember the new side of her – her hidden creative side of poetry and watercolors. Her face looks different. The more closely I look, the more her features bend and shift before my eyes.

A suffocating feeling rises, a vice that's squeezing my chest and working its way up to my throat. I gulp, trying to swallow and relax my throat. She's better but she could slip up. She looks fine right now, but what will tomorrow bring? Angry mom, happy mom, or emotionless, middle-grey mom?

The rest of them eat obliviously while I quietly trip out. Here I am, having a psychedelic experience (at least I think it might feel like one) watching Mom's features morph and melt while the rest of the family calmly chows on pizza. This can't be normal.

I eat quickly and excuse myself to study.

I spread my books and notes out on my bed and plop myself in the middle. I can't get my brain to focus; it's too busy spinning out on Mom.

Becky picks up on the first ring. "I was just going to call you," she says. "How's it going?"

"Peachy. I'm so knotted up I feel like I might puke."

"How's your Mom?"

"I don't know. That's what trips me out. I can't handle not knowing. How am I supposed to trust her again?"

"Take it one day at a time. That's all you can do. Even though you don't know how long or *if* she'll keep it together, you know *you* will be all right."

"I guess." I sigh.

"Look. Do yourself a favor. Just concentrate on you for now. Take care of yourself and let everything else go. Take a shower. That always helps me feel better. Try to relax. And get some sleep."

It's easier to relax with hot water raining on my head. The heat melts the aching feeling out of my temples. I contort slightly so the spray hits right behind my shoulder blades, right where my wings would be. I close my eyes and imagine the water is rinsing away all the tension and negative thoughts. I swear I almost see charcoal grey residue swirling down the drain.

The cool, crisp sheets on the bed feel incredibly soothing. It's only 8:30 pm but I can't keep my eyes open another second.

I don't dream.

chapter thirty-one

I get a healthy serving of déjà vu for breakfast the next day. Mom sets the table like she always does: there's a glass of orange juice at each place and a mug of steaming coffee for my father.

Except it's oddly quiet.

"Grab some cereal, guys, and have a seat," she calls from the kitchen. "Sausages are coming up." She sets a plate of them in the center of the table, and I sit transfixed by the tiny trails of vapor rising off of them while my brothers dive in.

"Dad will be down in a minute. Make sure you save a few for him."

I dimly hear her voice, talking to someone on the phone. Who can she be talking to this early in the morning?

"Yes, I was planning on going today," she says. "Mornings are usually better. 9:30 am? That would be perfect. See you then, Anita."

She returns with a steaming mug of coffee in her hand and sits at the table. I've never seen Mom sit for breakfast. "Anything good happening today?"

Brad, Charlie and I look at each other like, *who is this woman and what has she done with Mom?* Brad breaks the silence with an awkward clearing of his throat. "We've got our end-of-the-year class party this afternoon at Cauffield Park."

"It's a great day for that. Warm enough to swim," she offers. "Don't forget, you and Charlie have karate later." She sips her coffee. "I'm going to my first AA meeting."

Brad raises an eyebrow, then lowers his head back down to his plate.

"I signed an agreement at Silver Springs to go to meetings for the next year," Mom says. "I've also got a sponsor."

"Who is your sponsor?" I ask. Brad and Charlie continue to shove food into their mouths without stopping.

"Anita Brown, from the country club. You know, Amanda's mom."

Anita Brown is part of the crowd that lives on the beach all summer. Most days she's poolside, cultivating her tan in a red bikini. She's got leathery skin from all the sun exposure.

"That's great, Mom," I say in a tone I hope is

encouraging. "Have fun at your meeting."

She stares out the window for a long moment. Her hand gripping the coffee mug tightens. She takes a long shuddery breath, then nods absentmindedly and wanders into the pantry. Brad and Charlie vanish from the breakfast table.

I watch her walk away and a familiar sinking feeling swirls in my belly. How will I ever know if she's truly recovered and if she'll stay that way? I rinse breakfast crumbs and my panic away at the sink.

Moments later there are thuds and crashes overhead. Boys. Always wrestling. "Keep it down, you animals!" My mother yells at full volume from the opposite end of the house.

Thump! There's a sickening dull thud. A primal wail follows.

Heavy footsteps pound down the stairs. Brad screams, "Mom! Come quick! Charlie hit his head!"

"What have you done?" Her voice is quivery. "God damn it Brad, I've told you a million times…" Her voice trails off as she pounds up the stairs after Brad.

I run after her. Drops of blood trail across the rec room carpet. Mom cradles Charlie's head while Brad twists his hands. There's blood on the back of Charlie's head, staining the collar of his shirt. My breakfast surges into my throat. I am no good with blood; I'm already breaking out in a cold sweat. I quickly turn away.

"Easy, honey. It's going to be all right," Mom coos. "Brad, go get the first-aid kit."

Charlie won't stop crying, no matter how soothing Mom sounds. "Baby, you're going to be fine. I promise. We're going to clean you up and then I can assess."

Mom is completely calm when blood is involved. She's also excellent with injuries, accidents, broken bones, and pulling out loose teeth.

Watching her now, a stream of memories flashes through my mind. The time I shredded both shins when my doll carriage dragged me down a hill and she patched me up. The time Mike Wallace punched me in the nose and she fixed the swelling with a bag of frozen peas. Meals in bed on the "sick tray" when I was down with the flu.

Past overlaps present until my inner slideshow ends and I am back in this room watching her work.

Her hands. The same hands that were wrapped around Charlie's neck only two months ago, hell bent on squeezing the life out of him. Today her hands are healing hands. How can both things be true?

She rinses Charlie's head and gently dries it with a towel. "Okay, let me see." She lifts the back of the towel and peers at the wound. "It doesn't look deep. I'll give Dr. Peters a call and see if he has a minute to look at you."

Dr. Peters is a retired pediatrician who lives down the block. He's Mom's go-to guy for minor injuries. He gives her advice; she gives him homemade pastries in exchange. It's a win-win.

She draws Charlie into her lap and gives Brad the death-ray stare. "Tell me how this happened."

"It was an accident, Mom." Brad's voice cracks, betraying his nervousness. "We were playing, but it kinda turned into wrestling, and then his head connected with the corner of the table."

"I know you both know better. Brad, you're older and supposed to be setting an example. This kind of thing always ends badly and you know it." She blows a stray hair away from her eyes. "I'm going to have to think of a suitable punishment...for both of you. For now we can just be thankful everyone survived."

She picks up the phone. "All right. Dismissed."

Charlie crawls off her lap.

"Not you, mister. We have a date with Dr. Peters before you go anywhere." She looks at me. "Don't you have something to do?"

I hadn't realized I was staring. Open-mouthed.

I walk to my room slowly, thinking about the memories bubbling to the surface. Remembering them reminds me that both versions of my mother are true. It's just been so long since I've seen her loving, caring side. I want to hold on to those memories, collect them like pearls.

Maybe one day there will be a full strand.

When I return home from school I flip through the stack of mail on the counter. There's an intriguing envelope midway through the pile: rich, creamy paper with a gold embossed logo. I know what it is without looking at it. A quick glance at the return address confirms my suspicions.

I hesitate before opening it. The letter feels weighty in my hands, not just because of its actual weight, but because of the information it contains. This letter holds the key to my future: either a new life in New York, or staying here for another year.

I am afraid to look at it – no longer certain what I want – torn between going and staying. I stare at the kitchen wallpaper; at least the annoying strutting chickens know where they're headed.

I tear the envelope open, scanning for the one word that matters. I find it, third sentence down from the top. *Accepted.* I sit down heavily on the stool in front of me, still clutching the letter. I read it again and my emotions swim. I put it down on the counter in front of me and rest my spinning head on my hands.

"You're leaving me, aren't you?" My mother's voice comes from somewhere near my right elbow.

My eyes snap open. When I look at her there is pain all over her face.

"I knew it. I've known ever since I saw you dance at the Winter Concert."

"You were there?"

"Of course. I couldn't miss the chance to see you perform. You're my only girl. Growing up so fast... toward the life you've wanted for so long." She sighs.

"I just haven't wanted to face it. I didn't want to let go."
It is the closest thing to an apology from her.

We both have to let go now. Still, I feel like I've let her down in some way.

We look at each other for a long moment. And it's here in this glance that something ends and something new begins. Things between us will never be the same. I feel my new life, already becoming real, a new chapter blossoming thickly, unfolding in the space and silence between us, already pushing us apart.

This is a chapter I will write myself, without her help. I've already had to learn to live without it. She's in charge of her future. I can let go and let her choose her own ending.

But in this moment I am driven to close the space between us, at least for now, while I still can. I move in and give her a hug.

Miss Roberta sips her iced tea while I reread the NYSB schedule again for the millionth time: morning class every day at 10:00 am, followed by afternoon Variations at 2:30 pm and another class at 4:00 pm. Rehearsals. Somehow I'm also supposed to fit in school. And homework.

It's 3:30 pm and the little café down the street from the studio is almost empty. The skinny white-haired woman behind the counter is the only other person in here. I'm guessing she's the owner since she hasn't stopped vigorously polishing every surface since we got here. Her overenthusiastic cleaning is a funny contrast to the mellow Billie Holiday music playing in the background.

Miss Roberta put together this planning session after Mom called her with a million questions about details and logistics. I know my schedule is really complicated when even the family planner is having a panic attack.

"How am I ever going to make this schedule work?" I moan.

Miss Roberta stops sipping. "Simple. Block out all your ballet times first and fit everything else in the empty spaces."

I shake my head. It's painfully obvious there's not much time left over after I do that. "What about school? What about homework?"

"Relax," she says. "You are getting yourself all worked up over nothing. The Performing Arts School is only a few blocks away from the ballet studios. You can easily go back and forth. You'll go to first period in the morning, then morning ballet class. Return to school for a few more periods until your afternoon ballet classes."

I put my head in my hands. "My head is spinning." The thoughts tumble around like clothes in a dryer. I'm realizing I will barely have time to sleep.

She laughs. "It's nowhere near as hard as you think. You are lucky! In my day the school was downtown so I had to do almost all of my schoolwork on correspondence. I'd be at the ballet studio all day, then stay up all night trying to plod through boring textbooks and piles of homework. Let's just say I was not so good at keeping myself on track."

It's hard to imagine Miss Roberta ever being lax about anything. "How did you not go crazy? I feel like I might go crazy."

"You'll find your groove. Once you get into a routine you'll find you can take on more than you realized. You might even want to consider some private coaching or Pilates later in the fall."

I don't have the heart to tell her I think she's insane for suggesting I add another agenda item to my ridiculously packed schedule. I'd better pencil in some time to sleep before she finds a way to fill in those hours, too.

"Today's ballet students don't know how good they have it. There were no dorms when I was at NYSB. We had to find our own lodging and I ended up in some of the most bizarre living situations. First I lived with a crazy old lady who had eight cats; some of them would sneak in my room at night and poop on the floor. Then I lived in a women's boarding house for awhile – multiple floors of crazy old ladies – but a few of my ballet friends lived there too. Finally I got smart and rented an apartment with some friends, but three of us had to share the bedroom so we could afford the rent."

"Three people in one room?"

"It was chaotic, but fun. Certainly better than anywhere else I'd lived. Although there were always so many tights drying in the shower that it was hard to close the curtain, and then figuring out whose tights were whose..." She smiles. "But you do what you have to do to make things work."

So many details – it all feels overwhelming. I'll take history and world lit on correspondence. Sundays are our only free days. I'm afraid to ask Miss Roberta if I'm allowed to pencil in some fun. I already know the answer: there won't be time.

"I am so excited for you." She clasps my hands. "This is going to be such an amazing time in your life." Her eyes are shiny with tears. "Promise me one thing: that you will give this everything you've got. Work like you've never worked before. Go – and don't ever look back."

That's when I know that if I'm going to do this – really do this – I have to throw myself into my new life and let the rest go. I can almost hear the pieces of my life here breaking away into the dark void, like pebbles falling down a well.

She sniffles and sits up taller in her seat. "Look at the time. I've got to go. I'll see you in class later."

When I hug her goodbye, she's tiny in my embrace. It hits me then: she's been through all of this and come full circle. "Do you miss it?" I ask.

"All the time, my girl." She looks up and sighs. "All the time."

I watch her as she pulls open the front door to leave. My phone rings just as the tiny bells on the front door jingle.

"Sup, girlfriend?" Monique sounds happy.

"I'm holding the most important letter I've ever gotten. It's from NYSB. They want me, M. Full scholarship."

"Holy cannoli! Indy! You're in!"

"Yes. It's still hard to believe."

"New York. Such an amazing city…"

"You'll come visit, right?"

"Yeah, of course. Only—"

"Only what?"

"It's gonna be weird not having you around." Her voice is husky.

"I know." She's such a natural optimist, so when I hear the sadness in her voice the finality of my decision sinks in. My right eyelid starts this deranged, twitching dance out of nowhere.

She clears her throat quickly. "Well, we need to celebrate! Like, immediately!"

"We will. For sure."

"Have you told anyone else?"

"Only my family and Miss Roberta."

"What about Jesse?"

Good question. How am I ever going to tell him?

My eyelid twitches faster. "I have so much to figure out. I'll tell him. Soon."

Just as soon as I figure out what to say to him.

Chapter Thirty-Two

My backpack is loaded down with every last textbook I own. The straps cut into my shoulders and random square corners of books poke into my back. I force a big smile on my face as Becky pulls to a stop. The clouds and blue sky reflect on her windshield, so she looks like she's floating underwater or stuck in some faraway dreamland.

Monique does a happy dance as I squeeze myself and my bag into the front. "Eight more days to freedom!" She squeals.

"Bring on summer," Sarah returns. "Ooh, did I tell you? There's a thing next Friday night – everyone will be there."

"Don't you mean everyone from the *boys' soccer*

team?" Monique says.

"Who cares about them? Tommy's hosting. It's gonna be huge."

Listening to their banter, I already feel like an outsider, like I'm going through the motions of my life here, knowing it's about to be over. I should be happy, so why don't I feel that way? Is this aftershock? Now that the initial euphoria has worn off all I think about is everything I'm about to leave behind.

Today I'm going to let them know about New York. But how do I tell them I've chosen tutus and tiaras as my new best friends?

It's strangely silent. I look at my "people," these friends who have been an oasis in the middle of this life that's changing – even the parts I like best. It is bittersweet.

"What's bittersweet?" Becky asks.

Crap. Did I say that out loud?

"Oh, you know, that's when something is totally great and sad at the same time…get it? Part bitter, part sweet?" Sarah says.

"Thanks, Sarah. Got that part." Becky looks at me expectantly.

"So I got this letter yesterday—" My voice catches. Damn emotions. Wish I wasn't such a sap sometimes. I clear my throat and start again. "Not just any letter. *The* letter. The one I've been waiting for. The New York School of Ballet wants me and they've offered me a full scholarship."

Sarah squeals as she hugs me really hard.

"That was my ear." My left eardrum tingles when she pulls away.

Monique chimes in. "Like it could have gone any other way. Puh-*leeez*. I knew you would get accepted. You are officially a rock star."

And they're off. Chattering away, a million miles a minute, from 0 to 60 and beyond. I close my eyes and listen to the animated cacophony of their conversation, letting it wash over me like a giant wave.

Right here in the middle of their blissful pandemonium, I am home.

We brush through the crowded school hallways like salmon swimming upstream. This is the perfect metaphor for my life here, swimming in the opposite direction from the crowd. Everything feels heavy, especially my heart.

"Sleep much?" M says, looking at me with concern. "Because you look so tired everything is drooping – even the corners of your mouth."

"I hardly slept. Too much to think about."

"You need to chill this weekend."

"I can't. I have to—"

"In fact—" Her voice raises an octave, "—*in fact*, you are coming to lunch on Saturday afternoon to celebrate. I am not inviting. I'm insisting."

"I just don't see how—"

"Uh-uh. No you don't. I'm not taking no for an answer." She folds her arms across her chest with a little grunt.

There is no arguing with her. I opt for silence instead.

She gives a satisfied little nod. "Two o'clock. My place. Or else."

Fine. I'll have to bow out some other time when she's more capable of listening. She flounces off. I turn to my locker with a sigh. I cram in most of my books and slam the door closed. Flinch as I notice the figure in front of me.

Marlene James leans casually on the locker next to mine, her face strangely blank for a change. "I don't get it," she says, shaking her head.

I fold my arms and stare at her. Raise an eyebrow.

"I keep asking myself why. Why is it always you?" She looks at the floor. "You get everything. Ballet. Jesse—"

"That's the difference between you and me. I'm just living my life. It was never a competition for me." I notice how pale she is, the dark circles under her eyes. For just a moment I think about how she must feel and something in me softens. I don't know why but I want to say something to make her feel better—maybe it's an echo from the past when we were friends or compassion for her pain now. Either way, I want to help."Look, just take care of yourself."

Her face contorts into a scowl. "Why don't you just mind your own business?"

Or not.

I watch her retreat down the hall and shrug to myself. Some people may never get it. Not my problem.

The trail at Myer's Bridge is golden in the receding sun. Water gently laps at the shoreline, stirred up by a passing gust of wind. Jesse seats himself next to me. I sneak a glance at him. I want to run my fingers though his ruffled post-basketball tousled hair. I drink in his scent, part citrus, part spice, committing it to memory.

The grass itches the backs of my thighs. I want to drag out this part where I don't say anything for just a while longer. As long as I'm silent, I can sit in this crossroad with the past at my back, the future ahead, and this moment in between.

A flock of Canadian geese splashes in for a landing. They catch sight of us and paddle briskly across the lagoon, looking for handouts.

"Look at them," Jesse guffaws. "When they are after something they stick their necks out so far it's comical."

I try to laugh, but it comes out forced and weak.

"You okay?" He looks concerned. "You don't seem like yourself."

"I guess," I say. *My dreams are coming true but you're not in them.* How do you say that to someone without hurting them? "You know how I've been waiting to hear back from that ballet school in New York?"

He nods enthusiastically. "You've been talking about it for months. Did you hear from them?"

I nod, my eyes filling with tears. "Yeah." *I think I'm going to puke up the bowling ball in my stomach.* "I've been accepted...on scholarship."

He pulls me in for a hug. "Isn't this is what you've been waiting for? Why are you crying?"

The tears come faster. My throat feels raw and tight. I look at my hands, folded primly in my lap, because it's too painful to look him in the eye. "Everything is going to change. My life will be crazy – classes every day, school, rehearsals, homework, practically no free time."

"But New York isn't far. They have trains that go there, you know."

I shake my head. "I want to be with you but I have to give this everything I've got. I can't do both. It wouldn't be fair to you – to us."

He stares at me. "I thought you might try."

I nod mutely. My heart curls in on itself. "I wish there was another way. But I can't make it work. I'm sorry."

His jaw tightens. "I get it," he says quietly. "I hoped we'd have more time, or maybe you wouldn't get in...but of course you got in. They'd be crazy not to take you." He runs a hand through his hair. "I think I knew this would happen. But whenever I started to think about it, I'd push the thoughts away. Figured I could deal with it later."

I take his hand. Our fingers intertwine. "I think I did the same thing."

The sky fills with gold, peach, and pink as the light begins to fade. A single purple smear runs through it. I grip his hand more firmly.

He reaches behind his neck and places the bear's tooth necklace in my palm, folding his fingers over mine. "I want you to have this," he says, smiling at me. "I've had it a long time and I think you should have it now."

"Jesse, it's too much. I can't—"

"New York is a big place. It's brought me a lot of courage. I hope it does the same for you."

The tears come faster, plopping down on my hand that's holding the necklace. I sniffle loudly. "Thank you. It's like carrying a piece of you with me."

His lips brush the top of my head. "I will always be rooting for you. No matter what."

I feel it then: another piece of my life breaking away and spinning off into the void. Gone.

chapter thirty-three

The huge tower of textbooks on my desk is the tower of doom from which there is no escape. I feel like Rapunzel. Plus I am going cross-eyed from staring at books for so long.

"Indy!" Mom calls. She's at my door before I can answer. She glances at the stack of books. "Looks like a lot of work."

I can only sigh in response. "Exams always are. No way around it."

"You can't study every minute or you'll drive yourself nuts. Why don't you take a break?"

"What is this, a conspiracy? First Monique bugs me to take time off, now you. Exams start Monday."

She gives me a look. "No conspiracy here. Just people who care. When are you going to Monique's?"

"In twenty minutes. But I still have tons to do and now I'm regretting it."

"You have to eat sometime, don't you?"

"Don't go getting all logical on me."

"I'll make it easy," she says. "I officially refuse to make lunch for you today."

I stare at her. This peppy version of Mom I still don't get.

She raises an eyebrow. "Just go, okay? There's nothing wrong with taking an hour off."

I hate it when she's sensible. "All right, all right. I'll go. You people win."

"Good. Here's your clean laundry." She puts a stack of folded clothes on my bureau and dumps a mass of socks on my bed. "I draw the line at socks. You deal with it yourself." Delegation is another one of her new, annoying habits.

The sky is the pure azure blue of summer with not a single cloud as far the eye can see. It's such a beautiful day that I'm glad Mom forced me out of the house.

Of course I'll never admit that to her.

Monique flings the door open before I can knock. "Hey, you," she says. "Come on back, I set us up outside."

She leads the way, pausing dramatically at the French doors that open onto the back patio. A small smile percolates on her face.

"C'mon, slowpoke." She suddenly runs off into the garden like a madwoman.

"What the…?"

She's finally lost it. I follow her outside and blink at the transformation. Huge rainbow-colored bouquets of balloons sit on tabletops. Colorful streamers flutter in the wind. There's a long buffet table off to one side with silver chafing dishes emitting delicious aromas.

"Surprise!!!!" Figures pop out at me from all sides of the garden. Monique places a giant sparkly tiara on my head while the others throw showers of confetti. She skips back and forth, singing, "It's your birthday, it's your birthday-yay!!"

I've never been so surprised. Everyone is here: Becky, Sarah, and Austin stand with Bella and Rob. A bunch of girls from ballet class are in front of me and Miss Roberta wears the hugest grin I've ever seen, so large that it's a little alarming. Jesse stands off to the side, hands in his pockets, slouching in his usual relaxed way. My family is here, too. They must have sneaked through the back gate to get here before I did.

My heart swells so much it feels like it could sprout wings and fly away. Tears start flowing. *God, I am such a sap.*

"Surprised?" Monique asks.

"I can't believe you!" I say. "Crazy confetti queen! You need to be stopped!"

"In your dreams," she shoots back. There's a mischievous gleam in her eye. "I still can't believe you almost wouldn't come to your own surprise party. I had to call your mom and *beg* her to talk you into it, and even then we had to practically drag you over here. But you're here."

I hug her, hard. For once, we're both speechless.

"All righty, then. I need to go find my helper," she says with a wink. "Oh, Austin!" She scampers off.

Miss Roberta materializes at my side. "Well, my girl, you're on your way." A sad little smile flits across her face. "I knew you had it in you from the moment you walked into my studio." She laughs. "You and that little pixie hair cut of yours."

I roll my eyes. "I hated that haircut! Mom totally forced me to get it."

"I'm proud of you," she says. "And not just for getting accepted to NYSB."

I look at her and think about how she's been so many things for me. How much she's done.

"I couldn't have done it without your help. Thank you." I hug her and feel the burn of tears.

"You have everything you need inside of you. You always have." She fans her watery eyes with her hands to fight back the tears. "Good Lord. This is no time to cry. Say something funny. Quickly."

I laugh. Monique and Austin come out with a giant lavender cake covered in pale butter cream rosettes. Everyone starts singing and the world takes on an impressionistic wash through the blur of my tears. My people have gentle glowing outlines as they sing, their voices raised in unison.

How did I get so lucky? I think to myself. The thought surprises me. Six months ago I wouldn't have believed I'd ever feel this way. But now that I do, I'm grateful. I look at all of the people I care about, here in the same place, sharing this single point in time. It's a bit of a power trip – not the kind where you hold power over others, but the kind where there's power because of the people holding you.

Just then I'm struck with the irony that now when I am finally free to leave, there's a part of me that doesn't want to go...because of them. That's the thing about moving on; someone always gets left behind.

But even when you leave, a part of them comes with you and a part of you stays with them through the interconnectedness of shared memories and experiences. There's always hope for more in the future. Hope that the other person will aim high, take flight and live their dreams. Hope that this isn't goodbye, but merely farewell until our paths next cross. Hope that those paths will cross over and over again in a crazy zigzag pattern that envelopes the planet.

It's not too much to hope for.

about the author

photo by Julie Pavlowski Green

Since she was forced into ballet lessons at age five, **GRIER COOPER** has performed on three out of seven continents. Her first crush was in fifth grade but Tchaikovsky was her first real love. She left home at fourteen to study at the School of American Ballet but after living in New York City, San Francisco and Miami she's decided she prefers to live outside of cities. Today she lives in a somewhat secret seaside hamlet with her husband, daughter and Coco Chanel (a black standard poodle). She is a dance activist and recovered sugar addict. Find out more: **www.griercooper.com**

acknowledgments

A book is nothing without you, dear reader. Thank you for choosing to go on this journey with me. I hope you enjoyed it.

The creation of this book has been an adventure and I've met so many wonderful and helpful bookish people along the way. Thank you to Suzanne Lieurance, for guidance on writing careers, to Katherine Longshore for valuable input while this book was in its infancy, to Jen Swann Downey for wisdom on everything from pregnancy to publishing, and Angela Zusman for sage self-publishing advice. Thank you to Michelle Josette, for keen editing, and LJ Anderson at Mayhem Cover Creations for a truly awesome cover. Soul-searing gratitude to the finest, the best and most lovely critique partners EVER: Brandi Askin, Corina Vacco, Katherine Fields Rothchild, Heather Hughes, and Amanda Klase.

Unending love and kisses to my husband, Dash Forsyth, for believing in me and bringing me coffee in bed, rainbow-pony-powered love to Asha; thanks for being you. Love to the Newburyport Coops, the Wenham Coops and the Duxbury Coops, for repeated trips to the beach and endless summer fun and to Eleanor Downey Cooper for being fabulous. Thank you to my parents, Jay and Misty Cooper, for your love and support and the chance to pursue a dance career and to Chris and June Forsyth for adopting me with open arms.

Thank the heavens for the sisters I never had: Maria, Paula, Ann, Liz, Kellstress, Nanette, Brigitte, Lisa Wz, and the inestimable Nanci Starr, my bestest cuz. To Julia Lazar

Franco for spotting the talent in the room, I will miss you always. A special secret hand salute to Julie Pavlowski Green, creator of many gorgeous photos including my author photo.

Thank you to Krispin Sullivan, nutritionist extraordinaire, for keeping me healthy, to Sarah Powers for making yoga stick in my heart and mind, and to all of my teachers for showing up and sharing what they know.

Lastly, I am forever grateful to super-cool people who freely share what they know to help indie authors, most especially the following: Joel Friedlander, Joanna Penn, Gary Smailes, Mark Coker, Jeff Goins, J.A. Konrath, and Catherine Ryan Howard.

15792427R00155

Made in the USA
Middletown, DE
24 November 2014